How to Understand the Virgin Mary

Jacques Bur

How to Understand
the Virgin Mary

SCM PRESS LTD

Translated by John Bowden and Margaret Lydamore from the
French *Pour Comprendre la Vierge Marie*, published 1992 by
Les Editions du Cerf, 29 bd Latour-Maubourg, Paris.

Nihil obstat: Father Anton Cowan
Censor
Imprimatur: Monsignor Ralph Brown, V.G.
8th December, 1993. (Feast of the
Immaculate Conception of Our Lady.)

The *Nihil obstat* and *Imprimatur* are a declaration that a book or pamphlet is
considered to be free from doctrinal or moral error. It is not implied that
those who have granted the *Nihil obstat* and *Imprimatur* agree with the
contents, opinions or statements expressed.

334 02106 5

First published in English 1994 by SCM Press Ltd,
26–30 Tottenham Road, London N1 4BZ

Typeset at The Spartan Press Ltd, Lymington, Hants
and printed in Great Britain by Butler & Tanner Ltd,
Frome and London

Contents

Introduction: Mary, Mother of Christ and Type of the
    Church   vii

1. Mary and the Incarnation   1
2. Mary's Virginity   17
3. Mary's Holiness   37
    The Immaculate Conception   37
    Mary's Perpetual and Progressive Holiness   47
4. Mary and the Paschal Sacrifice   58
5. The Assumption of Mary   74
6. Mary and the Diffusion of Graces   96
7. The Cult of Mary and Appearances of Mary   113

Conclusion: Mary in the Economy of Salvation   132

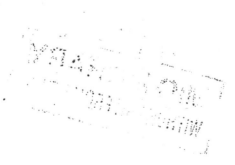

Introduction

Mary, Mother of Christ and Type of the Church

There are many ways of talking about the Virgin Mary. There are even people who will not discuss her, not through disagreement, but out of a sense of respect or religious sentiment. Of the hundreds of thousands of pilgrims who travel to Lourdes every year, for example, certainly very few feel the need to say why they make the journey, and some would not even consider themselves believers. And amongst the most devoted, many are regular in their praise of Mary (in saying the rosary, or Hail Mary) without ever thinking about what they are doing. The person of Mary has given rise to a huge diversity of devotions and prayers, pilgrimages, works of art, congregations, and popular or learned books.

Amongst Christians themselves, some people have wanted to contrast Catholics and Orthodox, who accord an important place to Mary in their liturgy and theology, with Protestants, who are less demonstrative in this area. And it is a fact that in recent years many Catholics have sought to go back to a simpler faith, centred on Christ, by abandoning, whether consciously or not, all marian devotion that they deem to be excessive, whether because it is felt too emotional, too 'popular', or too removed from the great paschal mystery of Christ.

At the present time, if only because Christians have never really lost their traditional attachment to Mary, an equilibrium is being re-established. With the passage of time, criticisms are sorting themselves out and the strong points are emerging even more clearly. The discussions will at least have served to demonstrate a faith that is truly evangelical as well as traditional. For it is impossible to read the gospel without encountering Mary in one way or another: before and in the incarnation, in public life (listening to the word and accepting signs of salvation), at the cross and at Pentecost. And to meet her is to understand her part in the truth: the richness of faith as commitment to the mystery of Jesus, fully man and fully God.

This book is unembellished and straightforward. It keeps to the essential task of presenting Mary as mother of her Son. Her important role is that she is a mother, and that is no small thing. The style is a simple one, firmly theological: sorting out what is authentic and what is not on the subject of Mary as it relates to the faith of the Church. This has its source in scripture and is authentically attested by the apostolic witness which proclaims the tradition of the Church, in particular through the Fathers and the Councils (with an important place accorded to Vatican II) and the great statements of popes and bishops in dialogue with the work of the best theologians.

This procedure, of going back to basics, may sometimes seem austere to readers more accustomed to works of spirituality or enlightenment, but it will have the overwhelming advantage of making them more attentive to the arguments and allowing them to make an informed judgment, and their minds will be more open to go on thinking about and reflecting on the subject.

The faith gives us Christ as the only redeemer and the only mediator: 'For there is one God, and there is one mediator between God and men, the man Christ Jesus, who gave himself as a ransom for all' (I Tim. 2.5).

St Paul calls attention anew to the uniqueness of the redeemer by the parallel which he draws in the Letter to the Romans between Christ and Adam: 'For as by one man's disobedience many were made sinners, so by one man's obedience many will be made righteous' (Rom. 5.19).

If one keeps to these two tenets, Mary seems to have no role in the plan of salvation.

However, the same St Paul writes to the Galatians: 'But when the time had fully come, God sent forth his Son, born of woman, born under the law, to redeem those who were under the law, so that we might receive adoption as sons' (Gal. 4.4–5).

And so, to conform to the divine plan of salvation, the Son of God could not submit to the law and enter our history to redeem and sanctify us without being 'born of a woman'. In order to make us adopted sons, he, the eternal Son of God, had to become a man himself, our brother, having Mary for his mother.

That is what we proclaim in the Creed: 'For us men and for our salvation he came down from heaven. By the power of the Holy Spirit he became incarnate from the Virgin Mary, and was made man.'

This text from the Niceno-Constantinopolitan creed and the one from the Letter to the Galatians form the basis of our marian doctrine. They stand as an introduction to the chapter which Vatican II dedicated to the Virgin Mary in its Constitution on the Church (*Lumen Gentium*, 52).

On the other hand, Mary mother of Christ, who is head of the Church, can be considered worthy of a title in her own right as the first member of the Church.

Mary is the model, the 'type of the Church'. Her role as an icon of the Church has led to the insertion of marian doctrine into 'the expounding of the doctrine on the Church' (*Lumen Gentium*, 54).

In the introduction to this exposition, Vatican II, after considering Mary within the mystery of Christ (*Lumen Gentium*, 52), sets her within the mystery of the Church (53): 'Mary is clearly the mother of the members of Christ . . . since she has by her charity joined in bringing about the birth of believers in the Church, who are members of its head. Wherefore she is hailed as pre-eminent and as a wholly unique member of the Church, and as its type and outstanding model in faith and charity. The Catholic Church, taught by the Holy Spirit, honours her with filial affection and devotion as a most beloved mother.'

Paul VI promulgated this Constitution on the Church on 21 November 1964, proclaiming Mary 'mother of the Church'. In his turn, John Paul II introduced his encyclical *Redemptoris Mater* (25 March 1987) by recalling the preamble of Vatican II's doctrinal exposition on the Virgin Mary. He too showed that if Mary occupies a unique place in the economy of salvation, it is as both mother of the Redeemer and type of the Church.

We cannot consider Mary in relation to Christ without also considering her in relation to the Church.

In the light of Vatican II and of John Paul II's encyclical, we can say that Mary's motherhood, understood in the fullness of its christological and ecclesiological significance, is the first principle of marian theology. That is why we must not see 'mother of Christ' and 'type of the Church' as two distinct principles of marian theology, but as two indissoluble aspects of the same marian mystery, that of the person of Mary, who makes a specific intervention in the history of salvation.

Mary, as the mother of Christ, who is head of the Church, assumes the quality of being the first member of the Church. She has the right to the title of the most important member of the Church, and as such is the model, type, of the whole ecclesial body of Christ.

Throughout this study of Mary we shall adhere to this double perspective, christological and ecclesiological, of Mary as mother of Christ and type of the Church.

1

Mary and the Incarnation

Mother of God

The expression 'mother of God' is not found in the Bible. However, we read there that Jesus is the Son of God and that the Virgin Mary is the mother of Jesus. On the one hand the New Testament calls Mary 'mother of Jesus' (John 2.1); 'his mother' (Matt. 1.18; 2.11, 13, 20; 12.46; 13.55); 'mother of the Lord' (Luke 1.43); on the other hand, the son born to Mary is called there the Son of God. The angel of the annunciation says to Mary: 'The child to be born will be called holy, the Son of God' (Luke 1.35). And St Paul writes to the Galatians: 'God sent his Son, born of a woman' (Gal. 4.4).

So the term 'mother of God' does not appear either in the New Testament or in the patristic documents of the first centuries. However, the reality of the divine motherhood cannot be dissociated from the Christian faith: Mary is truly mother of Jesus, the true Son of God.

St Ignatius of Antioch, who was martyred in the year 107, wrote in his *Letter to the Ephesians*: 'Our God, Jesus Christ, was carried in Mary's womb' (*Ephesians* XVIII.2).

The title *theotokos*

From the third century onwards, the title *theotokos* was given to Mary. It means 'mother of God' or, more accurately, 'the one who gave birth to God'. Its use spread during the fourth century. St Gregory of Nazianzus, for example, wrote about 382: 'Anyone who does not recognize Mary as the mother of God is separated from the divinity' (*Theological Letters* 101.4).

We can see how the deepening of the mystery of Jesus, the mystery of the Son, led to a questioning of the mystery of his mother.

If Jesus is one and the same divine being, the Son, having two distinct natures, divine and human, then Mary, in giving human life to the person of the Son of God, gave birth to God himself, in the person of his Son.

That is why when Nestorius, patriarch of Constantinople (428), rejected the title *theotokos* in his preaching, he provoked a lively reaction. For surely to deny that Mary is the mother of God is to deny the unity of Christ as one and the same divine being, that of the Son?

In effect, Nestorius allowed two subjects or persons in Christ, corresponding to the two natures, divine and human, united morally: the divine being begotten for all eternity by the Father, and the human person borne in history by Mary. For Nestorius it follows that Mary cannot be called 'mother of God'. She is only the mother of a human being, the mother of Christ, who was a human being: *christotokos*.

> If anyone does not confess that the Emmanuel is truly God and that for this reason the Holy Virgin is mother of God (since she bore in the flesh the Word of God made flesh), let him be anathema.
>
> Cyril of Alexandria, *First Anathema against Nestorius*

> We do not say that first an ordinary man was born of the Holy Virgin and then the Word descended upon him, but we say that having come forth from his mother's womb united with the flesh, he accepted a carnal birth, because he claims this carnal birth as his own . . . so the Holy Fathers did not hesitate to call the Holy Virgin Mother of God.
>
> Cyril of Alexandria, *Second Letter to Nestorius*

St Cyril, Bishop of Alexandria from 412, argued violently with Nestorius.

The Council of Ephesus (431) which deposed Nestorius did not, however, take up Cyril's anathemas against him.

So the term *theotokos* was adopted by the Council of Ephesus without being made into a definite dogma.

Following this, several bishops and several councils recognized Cyril's anathemas as the authentic expression of Christian faith. From that time the title *theotokos* assumed the weight of a dogma and was recognized as such by the whole Christian community. It was reinforced by the definition of the Council of Chalcedon in 451 and by the second Council of Constantinople in 553.

Mary, guardian of the doctrine of the incarnation

The divine motherhood of Mary has become the touchstone of christological orthodoxy, because the doctrine of motherhood is inseparable from that of the incarnation. History shows that the two doctrines are linked together, since to deny divine motherhood is to deny the doctrine of the incarnation and to question the doctrine of the incarnation amounts to a denial of divine motherhood. The result of acknowledging Mary as mother of God is to admit that she gave birth to a divine being within a genuine human nature.

In affirming that Mary is the mother of God, one is necessarily affirming that there are two real natures in Jesus Christ, divine and human, substantially united in a single divine being. This union of persons is called the 'hypostatic union', that is to say, the union of two natures in a single person.

That is the view of John Paul II's encyclical *Redemptoris Mater*: 'The dogma of the divine motherhood of Mary was for the Council of Ephesus and is for the Church like a seal upon the dogma of the Incarnation, in which the Word truly assumes human nature into the unity of his person, without cancelling out that nature' (*Redemptoris Mater*, 4).

In this way the Virgin Mary is, as Cardinal Newman put it, the guardian of the doctrine of the incarnation.

Virgin and Child giving a Blessing. The Apse, Torcello. Eleventh century.

The significance of divine motherhood

The traditional expression 'mother of God' needs to be explained, particularly to children who are learning the 'Hail Mary'.

Mary is not a divine person. There is nothing of the mother in God. Mary is not associated with God in the Christian mystery as Juno is with Jupiter in the myths of ancient Rome.

Mary did not give birth to the Trinity

Mary did not give birth to the source of divinity. We must be clear that Mary is the mother of the divine person of the Son only, and not of the whole Trinity.

But Mary truly gave birth to the human life of the eternal Son of God. Mary may not have borne the Son of God in his divine nature, but she certainly bore him in his human nature. The same divine being is at once the Son of God according to his divinity and the son of Mary according to his humanity.

Human generation results in a particular person

To understand this affirmation of faith, we must emphasize the fact that the human generation has as its end-result the particular person who is engendered. Motherhood is not limited to bringing into the world the body of a child which a woman has carried inside herself. A mother is the mother of a particular being, a little Peter or a little Pauline. In the same way Mary is the mother of the divine person of the Son, although she has given to the God-Man no more than his humanity.

If Mary did not give birth to the source of divinity, neither was her child an abstract being without personal subsistence. She brought a physical being into the world, the eternal Son of God, who, by entering into history, became her son according to the flesh.

Mary, on whom God's favour rests

Mary received the grace which is the badge of divine motherhood. At the annunciation, the angel came to her and said, 'Hail, O favoured one, the Lord is with you!' (Luke 1.28). Mary enjoys God's favour: in Greek the word is *kecharitōmenē*, which means literally 'favoured'. In the Old Testament the term is derived from the word grace.

The favour of motherhood

The word *kecharitōmenē* does not, however, explicitly reveal the fullness of the sanctifying grace accorded to Mary from her Immaculate Conception. Here it denotes the grace of her motherhood: 'Do not be afraid, Mary, for you have found favour with God. And behold, you will conceive in your womb and bear a son, and you shall call his name Jesus' (Luke 1.30f.).

A favour rested on Mary which singled her out from among all the other human beings beloved of God. Her election is summed up in the word *kecharitōmenē*.

The highest grace

The worth of a living being is the greater, the closer it is to God.

Now in the order of grace defined as a relationship of union to God, Mary received through her divine motherhood the highest grace ever accorded to a human being.

Of course only Jesus, as a divine person incarnate, was perfectly united to God to the point of subsisting in the divine person of the Son through a substantial union which theologians call the grace of hypostatic union.

But after the grace of hypostatic union reserved for Christ comes the grace of the divine motherhood of Mary, which is in the first rank of the graces of the union of God to a human being.

Mary is united with God not only by the grace of a spiritual filiation, but also through a real motherhood in the flesh.

The Annunciation. Fra Angelico. Museum of S. Marco, Florence.

The sanctifying grace of divine adoptive filiation

As we shall see, this maternal relationship with God resulted for her in an incomparable sanctifying grace, which she received at the time of her Immaculate Conception. Because of the grace of her divine motherhood, Mary, in the order of grace of divine filial adoption, is the foremost 'daughter of God'.

All Mary's graces and all her privileges flow from the ineffable grace of her motherhood. As the great doctors of the Middle Ages said: 'Do you want to know who this mother is? Ask first of all, who is this Son.'

Mary's predestination

The grace of Mary's divine motherhood presupposes a divine election.

Mary's divine predestination to become the mother of Christ is correlative to the eternal predestination of the Son of God incarnate in Mary for our salvation. Vatican II's Dogmatic Constitution states: 'The predestination of the Blessed Virgin as Mother of God was associated with the incarnation of the Divine word: in the designs of divine Providence she was the

---

'Blessed be the God and Father of our Lord Jesus Christ, who has blessed us in Christ with every spiritual blessing in the heavenly places' (Eph. 1.3). These words of the Letter to the Ephesians reveal the eternal design of God the Father, his plan of man's salvation in Christ. It is a universal plan, which concerns all men and women created in the image and likeness of God (cf. Gen. 1.26). Just as all are included in the creative work of God 'in the beginning', so all are eternally included in the divine plan of salvation, which is to be completely revealed, in the 'fullness of time', with the final coming of Christ. In fact, the God who is the 'Father of our Lord Jesus Christ' – these are the next words of the same Letter – 'chose us in him before the foundation of the world, that we should be holy and blameless before him. He destined us in love to be his sons through Jesus Christ . . .'

The divine plan of salvation – which was fully revealed to us with the coming of Christ – is eternal. And according to the teaching contained in the Letter just quoted and in other Pauline Letters (cf. Col. 1.12–14; Rom 3.4; Gal. 3.13; II Cor. 5.18–29), it is also eternally linked to Christ. It includes everyone, but it reserves a special place for the 'woman' who is the Mother of him to whom the Father has entrusted the work of salvation . . .

When we read that the messenger addresses Mary as 'full of grace', the Gospel context, which mingles revelations and ancient promises, enables us to understand that among all the 'spiritual blessings in Christ' this is a special 'blessing'. In the mystery of Christ she is present even 'before the creation of the world', as the one whom the Father 'has chosen' as Mother of his Son in the Incarnation. And, what is more, together with the Father, the Son has chosen her, entrusting her eternally to the Spirit of holiness. In an entirely special and exceptional way Mary is united to Christ, and similarly she is eternally loved in this 'beloved Son', this Son who is of one being with the father, in whom is concentrated all the 'glory of grace'.

Redemptoris Mater, 7, 8

---

gracious mother of the divine Redeemer here on earth, and above all others and in a singular way the generous associate and humble handmaid of the Lord' (*Lumen Gentium*, 61).

In his encyclical *Redemptoris Mater*, John Paul II strongly emphasizes this predestination of Mary as being inseparable from that of Christ.

Liturgy resorts to a biblical description of the origins of eternal Wisdom, which it applies to Mary to glorify her predestination to divine motherhood. Mary was present in the mind of God from the very beginning: 'The Lord created me at the beginning of his work, the first of his acts of old. Ages ago I was set up, at the first, before the beginning of the earth' (Prov. 8.22–23, from the first reading for the festival of the Presentation of Mary, 21 November).

Mary's maternal function

What role did Mary play through her motherhood in the economy of our salvation?

First of all, through her physical motherhood, through giving birth in the flesh, Mary contributed to the whole process of our redemption and sanctification.

The priestly mediation of Christ with the Father

At once God and man, Christ has been made mediator between God and humankind, thanks to the union of his divine and human nature in a single divine person. This grace of union consecrates Jesus as sovereign priest, and accredits him before the Father as the perfect representative of humanity, of which he is the head.

In becoming flesh, the Son of God enters human history; he becomes one with all humanity; he takes charge of us to redeem us.

By his very nature, Christ is already reconciling human beings with God in himself even before he has perfected his work of salvation; he does this through his teaching, through his miracles, his work of forgiveness, the gift of himself even to the cross and resurrection.

Mary's maternal role

Now who gave this human nature to the Son of God which made him our mediator with the Father? The Virgin Mary.

If the Son of God, to become incarnate, had not been born of Mary, he would not have been truly man, one of us, our human brother.

The Son of God desired to take flesh in Mary so that he could really enter human history and belong fully to our species by giving himself an ancestry like all other men and women. That is why, in their Gospels, Matthew and Luke attach such importance to the genealogy of Jesus.

So that Jesus could encapsulate the whole of humanity within himself, it was necessary for him to enter human history by a biological human birth. The incarnation is a mystery of immanence, immanence at the heart of the worldly human history of the God who is eternal and transcendent.

Through her motherhood, Mary confirms and signifies this immanence of the incarnation. We shall see later that the virginal realization of her motherhood bears witness to and manifests the transcendence of the divine being who has taken flesh within her.

Thanks to Mary, Jesus is truly 'Emmanuel', 'God with us'. In Jesus, one person of the Trinity is truly made one of humankind. If Jesus, as man, is not merely like us, but is also one among us, and as such is called to represent us before God through his ties of blood and equally to pass on to us his divinity through his participation in human life, we owe this too to Mary. Mary is 'the woman' through whom Christ has become, through this human solidarity, our mediator *par excellence* with the Father.

We can clearly see, therefore, how Mary, through her physical motherhood, contributed to the accomplishment of our salvation.

In this way, the Virgin Mary closely influences the mediation of Christ. As the mother of the unique mediator between the Father and us, Mary too, through her motherhood, takes on the role of intercessor, in which she appears before Jesus.

This maternal mediation of Mary, which is distinct from the mediation of Jesus, does make her a new intermediary between the mediation of Christ with the Father and us; she does not distance Jesus from us. On the contrary, the maternal mediation of Mary is the method chosen by God so that on the one hand his Son shares in our human condition and is fully our brother, and on the other hand in him and through him, humankind has a direct approach to God.

Mary's maternal 'Yes'

The motherhood of Mary is not limited to the biological process of giving birth, since it carries with it a psychological and spiritual dimension. Mary did not become mother of God in a purely fleshly way, in the sense that God only found his human body through her. Mary's motherhood involved the whole of her soul, her will, her intelligence, her heart, her whole being.

Although Mary did not initiate the incarnation, she was not presented with a *fait accompli*. She freely accepted the role of mother of Christ; she agreed to it freely with a maternal 'Yes' which made her the recipient of a grace with which she co-operated.

Vatican II puts a strong emphasis on this free consent of Mary, given at the time of the annunciation: 'The Father of mercies willed that the Incarnation should be preceded by assent on the part of the predestined mother' (*Lumen Gentium*, 56). 'And Mary said, "Behold, I am the handmaid of the Lord; let it be to me according to your word." And the angel departed from her' (Luke 1.38).

Mary's faith can also be compared to that of Abraham, whom Saint Paul calls 'our father in faith' (cf. Rom 4.12). In the salvific economy of God's revelation, Abraham's faith constitutes the beginning of the Old Covenant; Mary's faith at the Annunciation inaugurates the New Covenant. Just as Abraham 'in hope believed against hope, that he should become the father of many nations' (cf. Rom. 4.18), so Mary, at the Annunciation, having professed her virginity ('How shall this be, since I have no husband?'), believed that through the power of the Most High, by the power of the Holy Spirit, she would become the Mother of God's Son in accordance with the angel's revelation: 'The child to be born will be called holy, the Son of God' (Luke 15).

Redemptoris Mater, 14

God made a request of Mary by asking for her free co-operation; he did not make use of her as an impersonal instrument, having no will of her own. The act of faith by which Mary responded to God was a consequence of the grace of her personal vocation. Mary abandoned herself freely to the will of God, which did no violence to her inmost being.

As St Augustine said: 'Through her faith, Mary conceived Christ in her spirit before she gave birth to him through her body' (Sermon 215).

Vatican II took up this patristic theme: 'The Virgin Mary, at the message of the angel, received the Word of God in her heart and in her body' (*Lumen Gentium*, 53). And John Paul II, in his encyclical *Remptoris Mater*, compared the faith of Mary with that of Abraham.

Responsible human motherhood

Mary was not therefore mother only in the flesh, but after the spirit. Mary was an authentic mother, in the most noble sense of a truly responsible human motherhood. Even if she did not have physical intercourse with Joseph in order to become a mother (and that is the meaning of her virginal motherhood), she freely and consciously accepted her motherhood. We are therefore talking of a truly responsible motherhood.

True human motherhood presupposes a spiritual act on the part of the mother who gives birth. Mary achieved that. Human generation is not simply reproduction of the species: she gave life to a child who was an immortal, spiritual being, having reason and free will.

It is necessary, therefore, that the originator of this birth, the mother, should equally be a human being in the same mould, having conscience and free will. In human beings, the spirit must dominate the body, and this mastery of the spirit must exist even in the sexual act of generation.

Obviously sin can break up this harmony of body and spirit. Sometimes the woman has none of the spiritual control which marks human birth. She can only content herself, like a human being, in obeying the laws of the species. But it is the divine intention of the creator that the child be born of a love which is both physical and spiritual.

If, then, God wanted to be born of a mother, it is understandable that he should have sought out this most perfect human motherhood possible: a conscious, self-willed motherhood inspired by the deepest feelings which the mystery of motherhood can stir in the human heart. It is only through this that human motherhood can be used by God for his incarnation.

'Blessed among all women'

Without this moral and spiritual aspect, Mary's motherhood would not have been the incomparable favour which made of her a woman 'blessed among all women'.

Elizabeth's greeting

On the occasion of Mary's visit, Elizabeth's greeting, enshrined in the *Ave Maria*, praises

The Visitation. Catalan. Twelfth century.

10

Mary's faith, recognizing that the greatness of her motherhood lies in her faith: 'Blessed are you among women . . . And blessed is she who believed that there would be a fulfilment of what was spoken to her from the Lord' (Luke 1.42–45).

Unlike Zechariah, who did not believe the announcement of the birth of John the Baptist (Luke 1.20), Mary is blessed as one who believes.

This greeting of Elizabeth is recalled by Vatican II (*Lumen Gentium*, 57) and dwelt on by John Paul II (*Redemptoris Mater*, 20).

Jesus and his mother

Jesus, too, exalts his mother's faith by declaring how blessed are those who hear the word of the Lord and keep it: 'A woman in the crowd raised her voice and said to him, "Blessed is the womb that bore you, and the breasts that you sucked!" But he said, "Blessed rather are those who hear the word of God and keep it!".' This text is mentioned both by Vatican II (*Lumen Gentium*, 58) and by John Paul II (*Redemptoris Mater*, 20).

> The purpose and distinctive mark of Scripture, as I have often said, is to announce a twofold doctrine about the Saviour: that he was always God and Son, being the Word, the splendour and the wisdom of the Father; and that later, for us, having taken flesh of the Virgin Mary, the mother of God, he was made man.
>
> St Athanasius, *Third Discourse against the Arians*

The bodily motherhood of Mary attains its true greatness in the liveliness of her faith and the strength of her obedience to the will of God.

When the crowd told Jesus that his parents were looking for him, he said to them: '"Who are my mother and my brothers?" And looking around on those who sat about him, he said, "Here are my mother and my brothers! Whoever does the will of God is my brother, and sister, and mother"' (Mark 3.33–35).

Jesus' reply does not distance him from his mother, or belittle her. On the contrary, it enhances the eminent dignity of her motherhood, which relates to the holiness of her obedience to God.

Mother of the Redeemer as Redeemer

Considered in the perspective of responsible motherhood, with its maternal consent Mary's motherhood attains a dimension which goes beyond that of all other maternal consent.

In reality, a woman's consent to become a mother is usually given without all the facts being known: mothers-to-be do not know the futures of their children. Although, through the education that they give them, they are in part responsible for these futures, they can never respond fully to their action in bringing them into the world. A mother's destiny is always to a greater or lesser degree separate from that of her child.

The mother, associate of the Redeemer

But Jesus is Mary's gift in quite another way. The child to whom she gives birth is a pre-existent person who has existed before all time, the Son of God who finally takes flesh within her to redeem all humankind. He is predestined to be the mediator, the redeemer, the leader of all humankind.

Mary's free response therefore had to take into account the intention of the Son of God in entering into her. It was the Son of God's free choice to come as saviour of humanity which Mary freely accepted.

Mary was already a participant in her son's plan, and what made her different from other mothers was that, from the time of the incarnation and for ever afterwards, she linked her destiny with his. As Vatican II proclaimed, she is 'united to him by a close and indissoluble tie' (*Lumen Gentium*, 53).

Since Jesus is both a private and individual and a public personality charged with a mission, Mary is present to Jesus as a mother and as an associate.

It is as Saviour that the Son of God was made incarnate; it is as Saviour that the Virgin Mary accepted the task of giving him birth. In bearing Jesus, Mary embraced her son's saving plan. Her 'Yes' to motherhood was therefore a 'Yes' to the redemption of the human race.

Consent to the redemption

It is certain that, at the time of the annunciation, Mary did not know all the aspects of the redeeming work. But it was enough that she realized that Jesus was the expected Messiah. She was familiar with the prophecies concerning him, and like all the Israelites who remained faithful to the Old Covenant, she prayed for him.

In Luke's narrative, the words used by the angel to announce the birth of Jesus clearly demonstrate his messianic status and the saving nature of his mission. Therefore Mary was able, with the help of divine grace, to fall in with the redeeming plan even though she did not know how it was going to work out.

Mary did not know everything, but she accepted everything. In faith, she committed herself, and submitted to the will of God.

In the end of the day, it is of little importance to us to know exactly what Mary understood at the moment of the annunciation. Since the incarnation was already a redeeming work both in itself and through its bias towards the cross, Mary's consent to the incarnation was, in itself, already an immediate commitment to the work of redemption.

This fiat of Mary – 'let it be to me' – was decisive, on the human level, for the accomplishment of the divine mystery. There is a complete harmony with the words of the Son, who, according to the Letter to the Hebrews, says to the Father as he comes into the world: 'Sacrifices and offering you have not desired, but a body you have prepared for me . . . Lo, I have come to do your will, O God' (Heb. 10.5–7). The mystery of the Incarnation was accomplished when Mary uttered her fiat: 'Let it be to me according to your word', which made possible, as far as it depended upon her in the divine plan, the granting of her Son's desire.

Redemptoris Mater, 13

Mary was freely and knowingly the mother of the Redeemer as Redeemer. She therefore contributed to our redemption.

This is what Vatican II stated: 'She conceived, brought forth, and nourished Christ, she presented him to the Father in the temple, shared her Son's suffering as he died on the cross. Thus, in a wholly singular way she cooperated by her obedience, faith, hope and burning charity in the work of the Saviour in restoring supernatural life to souls' (*Lumen Gentium*, 61).

Mary's maternal 'yes' has a saving dimension, because Mary, who is not a redeemer in the same way as Christ, by her maternal consent identified herself completely with the fulfilment of our redemption achieved by her son.

John Paul II emphasizes the harmony of Mary's maternal 'yes' with the priestly 'yes' of Jesus.

Consent which is the fruit of a redeeming grace

Mary's maternal co-operation is possible only in response to an allotted vocation, not absolutely necessary, but given through a divine predestination which is quite free. And Mary's 'yes' at the time of the annunciation was already the fruit of redeeming grace, granted to Mary in expectation of the merits of Jesus.

For his incarnation, God wanted Mary's free consent, and he wanted it so much and so deeply that he achieved it efficaciously by his grace. We see at the heart of the mystery the links between grace and freedom. Without embarking on philosophical and theological arguments, we need only remember that the angel's message was not a command which restricted her, but a gracious invitation.

Vatican II wrote: 'Committing herself wholeheartedly . . . to God's saving will, (Mary) devoted herself totally, as a handmaid of the Lord, to the person and work of her Son, under and with him, serving the mystery of redemption, by the grace of Almighty God. Rightly, therefore, the Fathers see Mary not merely as passively engaged by God, but as freely cooperating in the work of man's salvation through faith and obedience' (*Lumen Gentium*, 56).

A new Eve

'For,' as St Irenaeus says, 'being obedient, she became the cause of salvation for herself and for the whole human race.' Hence not a few of the early Fathers gladly assert, with Irenaeus, in

their preaching that 'the knot of Eve's disobedience was untied by Mary's obedience: what the virgin Eve bound through her disbelief, Mary loosened by her faith.' Comparing Mary with Eve, they call her 'mother of the living', and frequently claim: 'death through Eve, life through Mary' (*Lumen Gentium*, 56).

> Mary the Virgin was found obedient, saying: 'Behold the handmaid of the Lord: be it unto me according to thy word.' But Eve was disobedient, for she did not obey when as yet she was a virgin. And as Eve, having a husband, Adam, but being nevertheless as yet a virgin . . . having become disobedient was made the cause of death, both to herself and to the entire human race, so also did Mary, having a man betrothed and being nevertheless a virgin, by yielding obedience became the cause of salvation both to herself and to the human race. And on this account the law terms a woman betrothed to a man the wife of him who had betrothed her although she was yet a virgin; thus indicating the back-reference from Mary to Eve, because the bonds (of sin) could not be put asunder other than by an inversion of the process by which they had arisen. The knot of Eve's disobedience was loosed by the obedience of Mary. For what the virgin Eve had bound fast through unbelief the Virgin Mary set free through faith.
>
> Irenaeus [died c. 202–3], *Against the Heresies* III, 22, 4

The ecclesial dimension of Mary's maternal 'yes'

Until this point we have thought of Mary, through her motherhood, as being personally associated in the work of the Saviour. We must carry our analysis a little further and show how Mary, the 'type of the Church', is associated with the redemptive incarnation by her maternal

'yes', not only in her own name, because she is personally involved in the mystery of salvation, but also in the name of all humanity, because she is the representative of humanity before the Saviour, Christ the head.

By accepting her motherhood, Mary showed

The angel is waiting for your response; it is time for him to return to the God who sent him. O our sovereign, we too await the word of mercy, we wretched ones on whom a sentence of condemnation falls. Behold you are offered the price of our salvation; accept it and we shall be straightway delivered. We are all the work of the eternal Word of God and we must die, but say a word and we shall be recalled to life. This is the supplication addressed to you, O merciful Virgin, by the sorrowful Adam, exiled from heaven with his unfortunate posterity. This is the supplication of Abraham, the supplication of David. It is the constant prayer of all the other holy patriarchs, your fathers, who also live in the region covered with the shadows of death. It is the expectation of the entire universe prostrate at your knees. On the response which falls from your lips depends the consolation of the unhappy, the ransom of the captives, the liberation of the condemned, the salvation of all the sons of Adam, of all your race. O Virgin, hasten to give us this response . . . O our sovereign, speak the word that the earth, hell and heaven await. The king and Lord of all things himself awaits, with the same ardour with which he has desired your beauty, your consent that he has made the condition for the salvation of the world.

St Bernard, Homily on the *Missus est* IV, 8

her commitment to her son's work. Now this work of her son has as its goal the collective salvation of the whole of humanity. Through her maternal 'yes', Mary by this deed involved herself in a very real way with the fate of all humanity. Through this universal repercussion, her consent takes on an ecclesial dimension. It carries the weight not only of a personal commitment, demanded by her role as mother, but also of a collective commitment called forth by her role as representative of the whole church.

Mary, representative of all humanity

Mary is the one who assented to the incarnation on behalf of all humanity. She is the one in whom all humanity welcomed its Saviour. St Bernard talked about the message of the annunciation with touching lyricism in this connection.

In his *Summa Theologica*, Thomas Aquinas wrote: 'It brings out that a kind of spiritual marriage is taking place between the Son of God and human nature. The Virgin's consent, then, which was petitioned during the course of the announcement, stood for the consent of all men' (III ad q 30, a 1). Pope Leo XIII frequently cited this text of St Thomas in his marian encyclicals.

There are some people who believe that what we have here is a poetic theme without any doctrinal merit. In fact, it is the theme of the New Eve, traditional to the Church Fathers and much developed in the Middle Ages.

To say that Mary accepted the incarnation of the Word in the name of or in place of all humanity is to affirm even more explicitly than the Fathers did, but without going beyond their thinking, that Mary's obedience contributed to the salvation of all humanity.

Besides, St Thomas himself, in affirming in his *Summa Theologica* that the Virgin's consent was awaited in the name of all humanity, was only making more explicit what he had written in his *Commentary on the Sentences*: 'This consent was the act of one individual whose influence affected the salvation of a multitude, indeed of the whole human race' (3, *In libros Sententiarum*, d. III q 3, ad 2, sol. 2).

Because her consent had a universal significance, Mary was the one who represented all humanity. Because Mary affected the destiny of all humanity by her reply, she spoke in the name of this humanity. It is not necessary for her to have been fully aware of being the representative of the whole human race: she nevertheless exercises this function. Her consent to becoming the mother of the universal Redeemer has, in the eyes of God, the merit of being a collective response on the part of all humanity.

The Adoration of the Child Jesus. The Master of St Sebastian. 1490–95. Louvre, Paris.

Mary, 'daughter of Zion'

Mary is therefore a highly privileged person in whom the juncture between God and the whole human race is made real through the incarnation of the Word. She is the member of the human race in whom, through the grace of God, is concentrated all that humanity bore in her of holiness and desire for union with God.

From the very beginning, humanity had been awaiting 'the one who is to come'. But this desire could not be fulfilled until the Virgin was there to receive the Son of God into her immaculate womb. This young girl in her home at Nazareth responds to the most deeply held desire of humanity.

She sums up in herself the whole of the long messianic expectation of the Old Testament:

'She stands out among the poor and humble of the Lord, who confidently hope for and receive salvation from him. After a long period of waiting the times are fulfilled in her, the exalted Daughter of Sion and the new plan of salvation is established, when the Son of God has taken human nature from her, that he might in the mysteries of his flesh free man from sin' (*Lumen Gentium*, 55).

The nuptials of Christ and the Church

Mary gave her consent to the New Covenant and to the spiritual nuptials between Christ and the Church.

She is not the spouse, but the pure Virgin who welcomes him. In Mary, humanity is ready to contract a spiritual marriage with the Son of God. The Virgin stands in the place of humanity as the contracting partner. The nuptials of Christ and his Church are in this way first of all realized in Mary. In agreeing to her motherhood, Mary gives her consent to the union of Christ and the Church and also the consent of the whole Church to Christ, her bridegroom. Mary, in her role of first member of the Church, is empowered to unite the Church with Christ spiritually, in mystical nuptials. Mother of Christ, in this way she already becomes spiritual Bride. She is therefore the image of the whole Church, as the bride of Christ.

Mary, type of the Church

In this way we see how Mary, at the incarnation, while being the mother of Christ, and because she is the mother of Christ, is also the type of the Church. 'As St Ambrose taught, the mother of God is a type of the Church in the order of faith, charity, and perfect union with Christ' (*Lumen Gentium*, 63).

The first member of the Church, the mystical body of Christ, Mary, at the moment of the incarnation, represents the whole Church; this is capable, in Mary, of welcoming through faith the Christ, its divine head.

2

Mary's Virginity

The universal faith of the Church

Mary's virginity has not been proved in a scientific way. She was not made the object of a report by midwives or by a panel of medical experts set up by the Jewish authorities, as the apocryphal gospels would have us believe. Mary's virginity is attested to us by the biblical texts which, with the Church, we have to read in the light of its tradition, as expressed in the professions of faith.

Revealed truth

The authentic Gospels reveal Mary's virginity to us and make it a mystery bound up with that of the incarnation of the Son of God. At the time of the annunciation, to Mary's question, 'How can this be, since I have no husband?', the angel replies: 'The Holy Spirit will come upon you, and the power of the Most High will overshadow you; therefore the child to be born will be called holy, the Son of God' (Luke 1.34f.). Luke affirms the virginal conception of Jesus as a sign of his divine Sonship. But he also tells us that Jesus' virginal conception was unknown to other people: 'He was the son (it was supposed) of Joseph' (Luke 3.23).

How then did the apostles learn of this fact? Were they a party to Mary's confidences, or those of Jesus? It is possible. But it is enough for faith that they understood it, through the grace of divine revelation after Jesus' resurrection, as a truth implied by the recognition of Jesus' eternal divine Sonship.

The primitive faith of the Church

We have proof that, from the very beginnings of the Church, the mother of Jesus was called Virgin. This title was given to her well before that of 'mother of God'. Thus, for St Ignatius of Antioch, Jesus is 'truly born of a Virgin' (*Letter to the Smyrnaeans* I.1). He also says: 'Close your ears to those who speak to you without confessing Jesus the Christ, descendant of David and born of the Virgin Mary' (*Letter to the Trallians* IX.1). And again: 'The prince of this world is ignorant of the virginity of Mary, her lying-in and the death of the Lord: three outstanding mysteries wrought in the silence of God' (*Letter to the Ephesians* XIX.1).

The Fathers, beginning with St Justin, defend the messianic interpretation of Isaiah 7.14. They emphasize that the text has to be understood in the sense that the mother of Emmanuel conceived and gave birth to a child while remaining a virgin (Justin, *Dialogue with Trypho* 43.66–68; *Apology* 1.33; Irenaeus, *Against All the Heresies* III.21; Origen, *Against Celsus* 1.34).

Professions of faith

The oldest baptismal creeds profess 'Jesus Christ, born of the Virgin Mary'. Thus the so-called Apostles' Creed: 'And in Jesus Christ his only Son our Lord, who was conceived by the Holy Spirit, born of the Virgin Mary.'

In the fourth century the phrase *semper virgo*, 'ever virgin', was widely used. We can read in St Epiphanius' creed (around 374): 'We believe in the Son of God who, for us men and for our salvation, came down from heaven and became incarnate, that is to say was engendered perfectly by holy Mary, ever virgin, through the Holy Spirit; who was made man . . . without issuing from a man's seed.'

In its turn, the Niceno-Constantinopolitan creed of 381 affirms that 'By the power of the Holy Spirit he became incarnate of the Virgin Mary and was made man.'

The Council of Chalcedon (the fourth ecumenical council, in 451) was to say a little later of Jesus: 'Begotten of the Father before all ages as touching the Godhead, the same in the last days, for us and for our salvation, born from the Virgin Mary, as touching the manhood.'

The Second Council of Constantinople (the fifth ecumenical council, in 553) proclaimed Mary's permanent virginity.

The First Lateran Council (649), called by Pope Martin I to condemn the heresy of monothelitism, defended Mary's divine motherhood and perpetual virginity.

The profession of faith of the Fourth Lateran Council (the twelfth ecumenical council, in 1215) recognized 'The only Son of God . . . conceived

> If anyone does not confess, with all the Holy Fathers, that Mary, holy, ever-virgin and immaculate, is in the true sense Mother of God, who, at the end of the ages, without human seed, conceived specially and truly by the Holy Spirit God the Word himself, born of God the Father before all ages, and that she bore him without corruption to her virginity, remaining unchanged even after childbirth, let him be condemned.
>
> The Lateran Council under Martin I, 649

by Mary ever virgin by the power of the Holy Spirit.'

Finally, Paul IV's constitution *Cum quorundam*, in 1555, gave this call to order: 'By our holy authority . . . we require and warn to turn from their errors of dogma . . . those who hold either that Our Lord was not conceived in the flesh by the Holy Spirit, in the womb of the blessed and ever Virgin Mary, but that he was born like other men, and of the seed of Joseph . . . or that this same blessed Virgin Mary is not truly mother of God and did not live in virginal integrity before, during and for ever after her giving birth.'

Undoubtedly several of these declarations were made by provincial councils which do not command the infallibility of the *magisterium*, and if it is true that the professions of faith proclaim Mary's virginity, she was not made the object of any particular dogmatic definition. But all the texts cited bear witness to the fact that Mary's virginity is a truth of faith professed by the universal church, even if we take into account that it has not been defined dogmatically.

Many other truths of faith, among them the most important, have not been made the object of definition because they have never been called into question. This is the case with the redemption and the resurrection of Christ, articles of the creeds, but not objects of properly constituted dogmatic definitions. It would therefore be unreasonable to dispute Mary's virginity by giving as the sole reason this lack of a formal definition. Moreover, the whole liturgy bears

The Virgin. Catacombs of Priscilla. Third century.

witness to it, particularly in the eucharistic prayers and in the baptismal vows.

It is of course because it is a truth of faith that Mary's virginity is firmly recalled by Vatican II: 'In the mystery of the Church . . . the Blessed Virgin stands out in eminent and singular fashion as exemplar both of virgin and mother. Through her faith and obedience she gave birth on earth to the very Son of the Father, not through the knowledge of man but by the over-shadowing of the Holy Spirit' (*Lumen Gentium*, 63).

The virginal conception

Mary conceived her son without the intervention of a human father; her pregnancy was not the result of sexual intercourse with Joseph.

We have to say that this is a mystery which cannot be explained by a scientific approach. It does not make sense to explain this act as if it were the same as the parthenogenesis in animals known to biologists today.

In the period at which Jesus lived, a conception like this, without the intervention of a male partner, could only be interpreted as being supernatural.

A supernatural act

There are people today who would deny this supernatural act. But is not the incarnation of the Son of God in human form the most unheard-of supernatural act there could ever be? That God, himself the Uncreated, the absolute Supernatural, should actually have taken on our own created human nature – is not that a mystery which goes beyond the limits of unaided human reason?

As a German catechism for adults remarks, to exclude *a priori* the possibility of a virgin birth amounts to raising once again the question of God and his incarnation. 'Is what appears improbable to human beings impossible for God, or is it true that "with God nothing is impossible"' (Luke 1.37)?

It is true that God in his omnipotence does nothing which is contradictory and which does not make sense to our intelligence, enlightened as it is by the light of our faith. We shall see in due course that, far from being a senseless miracle, on the contrary the virginal conception of Jesus is rich in meaning.

Let us be quite clear that in attributing this virginal conception of Jesus to the Holy Spirit, the biblical revelation emphasizes the supernatural intervention of God in this miraculous generation. There is no question of carnal relations between Mary and the Holy Spirit by his taking on the form of a man in order to make Mary fruitful. Scriptural statements about the virginal conception of Jesus have nothing in common with pagan mythological narratives which tell of sexual intercourse between masculine gods and feminine creatures.

We must also note that, apart from the supernatural character of the virginal conception, the incarnation of the Son of God in Mary's womb took place without upsetting the natural laws of gestation. Mary carried Jesus for nine months, gave birth to him, and wrapped him in swaddling clothes. She fed him and watched over him as all mothers have done: 'And while they were there (in Bethlehem), the time came for her to be delivered. And she gave birth to her first-born son and wrapped him in swaddling cloths, and laid him in a manger' (Luke 2.6–7).

The Gospel of Luke

The two stories of the infancy of Jesus in Luke (1.26–38) and Matthew (1.18–25) suggest his virginal conception. Their texts are all the more convincing because they are different and independent of each other. But both contain the same affirmation of the virginal conception.

This is central in the account of the annunciation presented by Luke. To the question 'How can this be, since I am a virgin?', the angel replies: 'The Holy Spirit will come upon you, and the power of the Most High will overshadow you . . .' (Luke 1.34–35).

However, unlike Matthew, who puts it at the beginning of his Gospel, Luke presents the human genealogy of Jesus (3.23–38) only after he has reported his divine sonship in the account of the annunciation (Luke 1.35) and in the account of Jesus' baptism (Luke 3.22).

Now St Luke begins this genealogy of Jesus, which in his Gospel goes back from Joseph to Adam, by saying: 'He was the son, as was supposed, of Joseph . . .' (Luke 3.23). Luke takes care to affirm that he was not, while making the genealogy begin with Joseph, since the Old Testament establishes sonship only through males. Legally, Jesus, although conceived by the Holy Spirit, was son of Joseph and through him son of David, which was sufficient basis for his messianic legitimacy.

The Gospel of Matthew

Matthew begins his Gospel with the genealogy of Jesus. He traces it the other way round, from Abraham to Joseph, Mary's husband. But immediately after this human genealogy, the story of the announcement to Joseph expresses the faith of the Church in the virginal conception of Jesus: 'Now the birth of Jesus Christ took place in this way. When his mother Mary had been betrothed to Joseph, before they came together she was found to be with child of the Holy Spirit' (Matt. 1.18). Though Joseph is the legal father of Jesus, he is not his natural father.

However, here Matthew's problems differ from those of Luke. His first aim is not to demonstrate that Mary remained a virgin or that the virginal conception of Jesus is a sign of his divinity, but to bring out his Davidic sonship.

Matthew wants to teach that despite Jesus' virginal conception, he was quite legitimately the son of Joseph by David. Now Joseph, son of David, welcomes Jesus into his line, which has just been retraced in the genealogy, although Jesus has not issued from his flesh.

According to this story of the announcement to Joseph, Joseph, 'who was a just man', knowing that Mary was pregnant, 'and unwilling to put her to shame, resolved to divorce her quietly' (Matt. 1.19).

This decision by Joseph has long been interpreted as suggesting that, convinced that Mary had committed the sin of adultery, he resolved not to denounce her out of affection for her. Such an interpretation does not work, since Joseph was a 'just man'. So according to the Jewish law he should have sent her back and denounced her. That is why many exegetes today think that Joseph was convinced of Mary's innocence: he knew that she was pregnant through divine intervention, and felt unworthy to be the father of such a child and to take as his bride a woman chosen by God for the realization of a plan which was beyond him and in which he did not know that he had a part.

Then the angel of the Lord appeared in a dream and said to him: 'Joseph, son of David, do not fear to take Mary your wife, for that which is conceived in her is of the Holy Spirit; she will bear a son, and you shall call his name Jesus, for he will save his people from their sins' (Matt. 1.20–21).

The French biblical scholar Xavier Léon-Dufour interprets the passage like this: 'Do not fear to take Mary as your bride, since what has been engendered in her is of the Holy Spirit; you shall give him the name Jesus, which means saviour.' According to this interpretation the angel reveals to Joseph that even if Mary is pregnant by the intervention of the Holy Spirit, he has an important role to play: by giving this child his name he will convey Davidic sonship upon him.

So Joseph, the legitimate husband of Mary, was Jesus' legal father. Moreover it was believed that Jesus was the son of Joseph (Luke 3.23). During the hidden life of Jesus in the Holy Family Joseph had the role of head of the family and foster father of Jesus.

Belief in the virginal conception of Jesus, professed along with belief in the incarnation, does not prevent the Church in any way from celebrating each year the festival of the Holy Family. Joseph, in the Holy Family, fulfils the mission of the good husband, the good father, the protector, but he was also the one who educated Jesus, full of love and concern for this child sent by God. It is significant that interest in Joseph disappears once this mission has been accomplished. There is no question of it during the public life of Jesus.

However, let us return to Matthew's story. After this dream, 'when Joseph woke from sleep, he did as the Lord commanded him; he took his wife, but knew her not until she had borne a son; and he called his name Jesus' (Matt. 1.24–25).

Matthew reaffirms the virginity of Mary at the moment of the birth of Jesus. One is struck by this insistence of the evangelists Matthew and Luke on recalling the virginal conception of Jesus. This is one of the fundamental truths that they want to teach in their accounts of the infancy of Jesus, which are a doctrinal and theological prologue to their Gospels.

The name of Joseph does not even appear in the Gospel of Mark, which does not recount the infancy of Jesus.

It will be noted that if St Paul does not speak explicitly of the virginal conception, he speaks of Jesus as 'born of a woman, born under the law' (Gal. 4.4). To make us adopted sons, the eternal Son of God had to be born of a woman and be subject to the law. It is significant that in order to attest the human birth of Jesus and his subjection to the Jewish law Paul did not mention that Jesus also had to have a man as father.

In fact, if the virginal conception of Jesus is never explicitly mentioned in the New Testament outside the infancy Gospels, in them Jesus always appears as having no other filial relation than that which unites him to God the Father, his own Father.

Current objections

However, the virginal conception of Jesus has recently been objected to, not only by Protestants but also by Catholics.

Mary is said not to have been a virgin in the biological sense; only a moral and spiritual virginity is recognized for her, that of an eminent sanctity. The affirmations of the virginal conception in the infancy gospels of Jesus are said to derive from purely fictitious and symbolic accounts, without any objective reality. Luke and Matthew will have used this literary procedure to express the divine origin of Christ as the incarnate Word. They certainly say that the virginal conception is the sign of the divine Sonship of Christ. But this sign is not a real fact. It is a simple literary expression of the divine initiative which is at the origin of the incarnation.

These exegetes or theologians explain this purely symbolic interpretation by the influence of the cultural patterns which emerged either from Greek or oriental pagan sources or from the biblical sources of the Old Testament themselves.

Is there contamination from pagan myths?

The stories of the virginal conception are here said first to be the fruit of contamination by pagan myths. Indeed the mythologies contain numerous accounts of conjugal union between male deities and human females who give birth to demigods.

However, it is clear that the evangelists, like all Christians, found such pagan myths too

The Virgin. Catacombs of Priscilla, about AD 200.
Illustration of Isaiah 7.14: 'Behold, a Virgin shall conceive and bear a son,
and shall call his name Immanuel.'

repugnant to be inspired by them in their cate-
chesis on the incarnation.

It must be stressed above all that in the
accounts of Matthew and Luke the virginal
conception is not the foundation of Christ's
divinity but only its revealing sign. Jesus is not
God because, as in the ancient myths, he is the
fruit of sexual intercourse between a god and a
woman. But the virginal conception attests that
in Jesus the very person of the eternal Son of God
was humanly incarnate in Mary.

So influence from pagan culture is inadmis-
sible here.

Are the messianic prophecies of the Old Testament an influence?

On the other hand, could not Matthew and Luke
have been influenced by the prophetic texts of
the Old Testament which are thought to have
announced the virgin birth of the Messiah? In
that case Matthew and Luke would have been
influenced by prophecies that Jesus would be
born of a virgin.

As Matthew writes: 'All this took place to fulfil
what the Lord had spoken by the prophet:
"Behold, a virgin shall conceive and bear a son,

and his name shall be called Emmanuel" (which means, God with us)' (Matt. 1.22–23, citing Isa. 7.14).

Matthew quotes Isaiah from the Greek text, the Septuagint. This indeed speaks of the virgin, *parthenos*, who will conceive and bring forth a son.

But the Hebrew text reads: 'Behold, the young woman is with child and will bring forth a son'; it does not speak of a virgin but the young woman: *ha alma*. The Greek here has translated 'young woman' as 'virgin'.

In fact, in the Jewish world there was no expectation of a virginal conception of the Messiah. Matthew's interpretation of the prophecy of Isa. 7.14 as 'the virgin who will conceive' is not an attempt to respond to an Old Testament prophecy.

Many Church Fathers were to interpret Isa. 7.14, like Matthew, in terms of a virginal conception. Because they believed in it, like Matthew they wanted to justify this unusual fact by referring to Isaiah. So it is not the Isaiah prophecy which has influenced Matthew. On the contrary, it was the faith of Matthew, and then that of the Church Fathers, which led to the interpretation of Isaiah in terms of a virginal conception.

So the stories of Jesus' infancy which describe his virginal conception have not been shaped by the cultural influence of the Jewish world any more than they have been shaped by that of pagan mythologies.

These objections make Christian virginity meaningless

We might add that these present-day objections to the virginity of Mary are seriously detrimental to the status of Mary as an exemplar. If Mary is not a virgin, what could be the significance of the dedication to virginity of those who commit themselves to the religious life and priestly celibacy?

I shall be remarking later that this dedicated celibacy which bears witness to the incarnation of the Son of God denotes total surrender to Jesus and his mission. But if any member of the Church was to experience dedication to virginity and to offer this witness, was it not primarily Mary, by reason of her divine motherhood?

One might add that the expression 'virgin' currently used to denote Mary, 'the Virgin Mary', would itself become meaningless if these objections were valid. Does one say of a mother who has had a child that she is ever virgin? Must one say of every good mother that she is a holy virgin?

All in all, the affirmations of Matthew and Luke that Joseph was not the father of Jesus are irrefutable testimony, and are an inseparable element of the doctrinal teaching that the evangelists mean to give in this theological prologue, which is made up of the accounts of the infancy of Jesus.

If we want nevertheless to challenge the virginal conception as a real fact, there is nothing for it but to attribute the conception of Jesus to another father than Joseph, as Jews and rationalists still do, making Jesus a child born of adultery. But that is to enter the sphere of fable.

The significance of the virginal conception

The virginal conception of Jesus is thus well founded, in both scripture and tradition.

However, every revealed truth must have a significance accessible to our understanding when it is applied to the facts of faith. Many people reject this affirmation of the Creed *a priori* because they do not understand its significance.

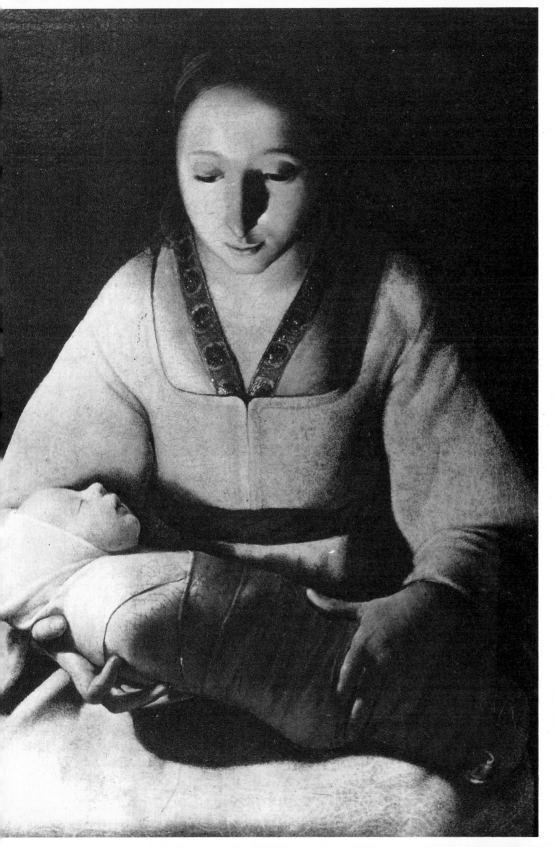

The Nativity.
Detail.
Georges de La Tour.
Museum of Rennes.

25

A pedagogical reason

It is not enough to invoke a pedagogical reason to explain the virginal conception, saying that if Jesus had had a human father it would be difficult to see him revealed as the only Son of the Father; that it was fitting that he could address only his heavenly Father as father, and therefore should not have any other father than God the Father.

An ontological reason

I think that there is a more fundamental justification for the virginal conception, of a strictly ontological order, which relates to the very being of Christ as the divine Word incarnate.

St Thomas Aquinas thought, and some theologians even today think, that the Son of God could have become incarnate after being conceived through sexual intercourse between Joseph and Mary. In that case the Word of God would have assumed human nature once he had become the fruit of this union. But would this not amount to a kind of abduction of the child by God?

The child born of a relationship of interpersonal love between a human father and a human mother is a human person. To have become incarnate, God would have had to have hindered this human personalization, putting the person of his own divine Son in this small human being born of the will of a man and a woman.

Today, in the light of personalist philosophy, which puts the emphasis on the personal relationship that formally constitutes the person, many theologians think that the fruit of an interpersonal relationship between two human persons, a human father and a human mother, is necessarily a human person who can become Son of God only by simple adoption. The fruit of a relationship between two human persons can only be a human person.

If Jesus had been born from sexual intercourse between Mary and Joseph, he would have been a simple human person, like any of us. As a gift of reciprocal conjugal love, how could Jesus not have been a new human person, issuing from this work of human love?

Jesus is the pure free gift of the Father

But Jesus is the free gift of the heavenly Father who has sent us his Son. In Jesus, God the Father has not given us a son born of a human couple, but has offered us his own Son, eternally begotten by him.

Certainly the eternal Son of God receives human life through Mary. But Mary merely welcomes into herself, by her own free consent, a pre-existent divine person. She welcomes him as a free gift of the love of God who took the initiative in his incarnation, and not as a human gift, the fruit of a human will.

That is the meaning of the prologue to the Gospel of John: 'To all those who welcomed him [the Word] gave power to become children of God, . . . who were born not of blood nor of the will of man, but of God' (John 1.12–13).

The reality of the incarnation

At all events, even if this question of the possibility of incarnation without virginal conception remains a matter of dispute, we have to see that the incarnation as it was was in fact brought about by a virginal motherhood.

According to the evangelists Luke and Matthew, and then according to the Church Fathers, the virginal conception of Jesus is the real testimony that Jesus is the Son of God incarnate.

The history of heresies from the Ebionites in the first century to the Modernists in the twentieth shows that the opponents of the virginal conception were also, for the most part, opponents of the divinity of Jesus, whom they recognized only as Son of God by adoption.

Conversely, we can see that those who have been committed to defending the virginity of

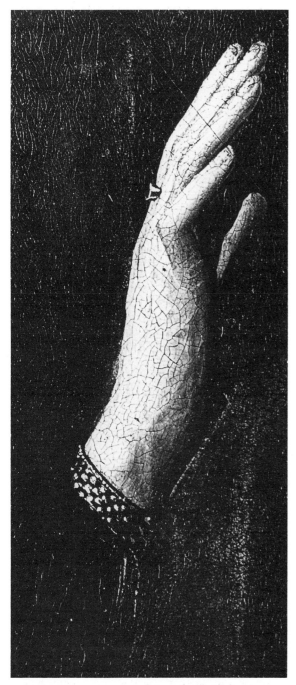

Married Love. Detail. Portrait of Arnolfini and his Wife, van Eyck. The National Gallery, London.

Mary, the mother, have done so principally in order to defend the divinity of Jesus, the Son. Even now we find a clearly adoptionist tendency among theologians who deny the virginal conception of Jesus.

The incarnation, mystery of transcendence and immanence

The incarnation is a mystery of both transcendence and immanence: the mystery of the transcendent God who, in becoming man, becomes immanent in human history.

To be completely immanent for the human race, the eternal Son of God was willing to be born of a human mother (Gal. 4.4).

However, this immanence must not veil the transcendence of the divine Word who became incarnate in Mary.

By her motherhood Mary brings about the immanence of the incarnation of the Son of God. The virginal conception safeguards and guarantees the transcendence of the divine incarnate person.

So the virginal motherhood of Mary is not bound up with mistrust of the sexual act which sees it as always being stained with sin. It was not to safeguard his perfect holiness that Jesus was conceived of a virgin, nor to preserve him from original sin, as was said following Augustine's explanation of the genetic transmission of original sin.

The spiritual significance of the virginity of Mary

To understand the significance of the virginity of Mary, it should be added that this is not only a biological reality but also has a profoundly spiritual character.

The virginity of Mary signifies total consecration to the Son of God whom she engenders as the free gift of God. To God who gives himself to her, Mary responds by abandoning herself totally to him. Mary's virginity is the sign of her perfect receptiveness to free grace from on high. That is why, as we shall see, Mary has remained virgin in perpetuity, and is always spoken of as Mary, *semper virgo*, 'ever virgin'.

Mary and the purpose of her virginity

Does that mean that we have to affirm that this perpetual virginity of Mary was the faithful fulfilment of a vow of virginity formulated even before she became betrothed to Joseph?

At the annunciation, when the angel has just said to Mary, 'You will conceive in your womb,' she asks, 'How can this be, since I am a virgin?' (Luke 1.31–34).

St Augustine and numerous Fathers interpreted this saying as a formal vow of virginity. Even now, some theologians accept that at this moment Mary is expressing her will to remain a virgin.

But literally, Mary says: 'How can that be since I do not know a man?' In this context, 'know' can have the biblical sense of having sexual intercourse. Mary, who is betrothed to Joseph, is still a virgin. The angel tells her that she is going to become a mother. She understands that this is to happen soon, as does Samson's mother when

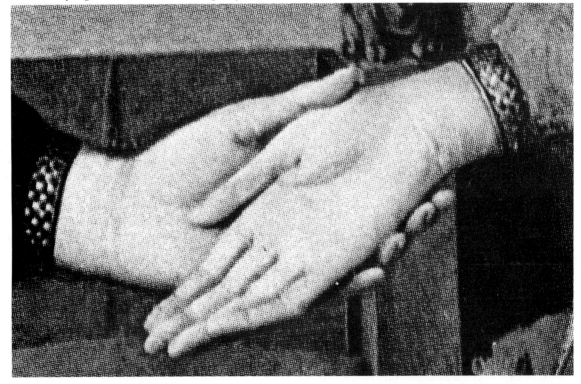

Married Love. Detail. Portrait of Arnolfini and his Wife, van Eyck. 1434. The National Gallery, London.

she is told of his impending birth (Judges 13.5–8).

So she is objecting that she has not had sexual intercourse with Joseph. She does not say that she does not mean to, because of a vow to virginity. The present tense of the verb indicates a state and not an intention, since it is hard to reconcile the reality of the marriage between Mary and Joseph with such a vow.

Virginal consecration at the moment of the incarnation

Thus it seems that Mary committed herself to virginity only from the time of the incarnation, so as to devote herself totally to this child which was coming to her from God. Her dedication to virginity went along with the consent that she gave to the incarnation.

By taking Marry into his home Joseph, too, joined in this plan of virginity which in fact, in the Church, only makes sense in terms of the incarnation. Among Christians, dedication to virginity is a testimony given to the incarnation of the Son of God, certainly incarnate in the flesh, but without being born of the will of the flesh. It is also a total consecration to Christ and his redemptive mission.

In the end, though, this question of the moment when Mary voluntarily made a vow to remain virgin remains a matter of dispute.

Unconditional abandonment to the will of God

At all events, as Karl Rahner writes, in her unreserved abandonment, following total availability to God lived throughout her life from her infancy, Mary had all the dignity of a chosen virgin. This is aroused and consciously formulated in her response in faith and abandonment to the grace of motherhood which is offered to her at the moment of the annunciation.

Virgin in giving birth

It is said of Mary that she remained virgin 'before, during and after giving birth'.

In fact this is always the same state of virginity. The commitment of her virginal motherhood, expressed at the moment when she consents to the message of the annunciation, will be renewed constantly all through her life. 'Mother of God, ever Virgin', is a title attributed to her by the Second Council of Constantinople (Fifth Ecumenical Council, 553).

The constitution of Paul IV, *Cum quorundam*, stated that 'Mary remained an intact virgin before, during and perpetually after giving birth.' Here Paul IV's text only expresses the fact of the persistence of the physical virginity of Mary in the act of giving birth, without explaining it physiologically.

In general, the Fathers and scholastic theologians understood this as the absence of any lesion and taught that Mary gave birth to Jesus in a miraculous way, without any wound and consequently without pain.

Two questions must be distinguished here: that of giving birth without pain and that of giving birth without breaking the physical seal of virginity.

Painless childbirth

The first question should not cause any difficulty today, since several forms of painless childbirth are recommended and practised.

However, it is not possible to evoke the testi-

The Nativity. Palermo. Twelfth century.

mony of scripture in affirming that Mary experienced a painless childbirth. The text which states that Mary 'gave birth to her firstborn son and wrapped him in swaddling cloths and laid him in a manger' (Luke 2.6–7) does not prove, as some have claimed, that this childbearing took place without pain or fatigue.

Still, there is nothing to stop us following the Fathers in thinking that, in becoming incarnate, God could spare his mother the pains of childbearing. Mary experienced many trials during her life and she suffered at the foot of the cross. But at the moment of giving birth she could very well have experienced motherhood as a purely joyous mystery, with no pain whatsoever.

As Pius XII said, the pains of childbirth are in any case not an expiatory consequence of original sin, imposed deliberately by God.

While it may not be a dogma of faith, the painless childbirth experienced by Mary is certainly a traditional teaching which today matches one of the aspirations of women's liberation. Mary provides the prototype of this painless childbirth which science offers to all women.

Physical integrity

The second question, that of the physical preservation of virginity without a rupture of the hymen, is much more delicate.

Many Church Fathers and, following them, doctors of the church, affirmed the reality of this physical integrity principally because it seemed to them to be the infallible and necessary sign of the absence of sexual relations.

At this period a man who married a girl sent her back if he found that she had been deflowered. That still happens today in many African or Arab countries.

But in our day, at least in our Western world, this physical preservation is no longer considered an infallible scientific proof, demanded as a sign of a life lived in virginity. There are women who have lost their physical integrity without ever having had sexual intercourse with a man.

Conversely, scientific journals have given cases of women who have been able to have sexual intercourse without breaking their hymen.

So the sign of physical integrity can no longer be a necessary element in the moral definition of virginity.

Besides, scripture attests the active role of the Virgin Mary in the act of giving birth (Matt. 1.25; Luke 2.7) without any indication that this is a miraculous event.

The apocryphal gospels invented the most fantastic stories, bringing in midwives who verify Mary's physical integrity with their hands. Their concern was to prove to those who denied the virginal conception of Jesus that Mary had no sexual intercourse either with Joseph or with any other man.

So the question is that of knowing whether by affirming the physical integrity of Mary the Fathers were attesting a revealed truth, Mary's virginity, by interpreting it, under this physical aspect, from an accepted scientific point of view of their time, but one which would be dubious today.

This question of the physical integrity of Mary in giving birth remains problematical. It is not the object of defined faith. However, the emphasis of a very old tradition on this point compels us to show a degree of prudence and even reserve in our affirmations. This question cannot be touched on in a peremptory fashion and needs to be treated carefully.

The spiritual significance of virginity in childbirth

Even if we do not pronounce on its anatomical aspect, we can at least put the emphasis on the profoundly spiritual significance of Mary's virginity in giving birth.

At the moment of giving birth Mary welcomed her child, not as the fruit of sexual relations with Joseph, but as the pure free gift of the Father. She welcomed him by offering herself to him in an act of virginal dedication.

By his birth, Jesus himself consecrated the virgin womb of his mother. He consecrated the virginity of Mary by making her motherhood a virgin motherhood.

Vatican II, which did not want to enter into gynaecological discussions, recalled that giving birth to Jesus did not diminish but consecrated the virginity of Mary. It speaks of the 'firstborn son who did not diminish his mother's virginal integrity but sanctified it' (*Lumen Gentium*, 57).

In bringing Jesus into the world, Mary does not lose the virginity by which she is consecrated to God at the moment of his incarnation in her. On the contrary, at the moment of her giving birth, Mary's virginity is sanctified by Jesus who comes forth from his mother's womb. As Louis Bouyer remarks, 'Mary's own grace is not simply that she is a virgin and the purest of virgins, but that she is virgin even in motherhood . . . Her virginity comes to full flower in her motherhood, which, far from limiting it, consummates it' (*Le Culte de la mère de Dieu*, Paris 1954, 15).

Virgin after childbirth

The virginity of Mary after the birth of Jesus means that she remained virgin and did not have other children. This virginity is understood as the extension of the 'yes' which she gave at the incarnation. Mary devoted herself wholly to Jesus and his mission in the history of salvation.

This virginity after childbirth is not explicitly affirmed by the texts of the Gospels. But one cannot derive any objection from them which would put it in question. The tradition is unanimous: very soon the perpetuity of Mary's virginity is mentioned whenever she is spoken of: Mary, *semper virgo*, 'ever virgin'.

The Fathers, in particular St Ambrose and St Augustine, reacted vigorously against those who denied this perpetual virginity.

The 'brothers of Jesus'

St Jerome refuted Helvidius, who put Mary forward as the model for mothers of large families by referring for support to the Gospels, which speak of 'Jesus' brothers': thus, in Matthew 12.46, 'While he was still speaking to the people, behold his mother and his brothers stood outside, asking to speak to him.'

But the Hebrew word *ah*, brother, has a broader meaning than in English or French. Among the Jews, as in many countries in Africa, Asia and Oceania today, 'brother' can denote not only the son of the same mother but half-brother, nephew, first and more distant cousin, kinsman generally and even compatriot (Gen. 13.8; 14.16; 29.15; Lev. 10.4; I Chron. 23.22).

In the Gospels we find positive indications that 'brother' has this wider meaning. In them several men who are called brothers of Jesus are also mentioned as sons of another Mary than the mother of Jesus; as in Mark 6.3: 'Is not this the carpenter, the son of Mary and the brother of James and Joses and Judas and Simon, and are not his sisters here with us?' Now James and Joses are certainly sons of another Mary, quite distinct from the mother of Jesus (John 2.1; 19.25).

This other Mary is called 'the mother of James the younger and of Joses' (Mark 15.40).

On Calvary, 'There were also many women there, looking on from afar . . . among whom were Mary Magdalene, and Mary the mother of James and Joseph, and the mother of the sons of Zebedee' (Matt. 27.55–56).

Then, after the burial of Jesus, 'Mary Magdalene and Mary the mother of Joses saw where he

was laid' (Mark 15.47). Finally, 'When the sabbath was past, Mary Magdalene, and Mary the mother of James, and Salome, brought spices, so that they might go and anoint him' (Mark 16.1).

These passages prove sufficiently that the term 'brothers of Jesus' is not to be interpreted in the narrowest sense.

Jesus, 'firstborn son'

Finally, let us note two objections which have been derived from Mark 2.7 and Matthew 1.25. Their arguments are still used by sectarian propagandists.

Mary 'gave birth to her firstborn son' (Luke 2.7). So will she have had other children, since Jesus is said to have been the first? Among the Jews, the term 'firstborn' denotes the child which was the first to open the mother's womb, which belonged to God and had to be redeemed by an offering. The epithet 'firstborn' used by Luke to denote Jesus at the moment of his birth (Luke 2.7) is doubtless meant to prepare for the application to Jesus of the law of Exodus 13.2, 13, when he is presented in the Temple. 'They brought him up to Jerusalem to present him to the Lord (as it is written in the law of the Lord, "Every male that opens the womb shall be called holy to the Lord") and to offer a sacrifice according to what is said in the law of the Lord, "A pair of turtledoves, or two young pigeons"' (Luke 2.22–24).

Luke uses the term 'firstborn', which is understood and known universally. This title does not imply that there were further children after the first.

We should note an interesting fact: a Jewish inscription has been found in Egypt, apparently dating from the time of Augustus. It is the epitaph of a mother who died in the pangs of giving birth to her 'firstborn' son. So in this case the term is used for a child who will remain unique.

Another objection drawn from scripture

Another objection is drawn from Matthew 1.25: 'Joseph took his wife, but knew her not until he had borne a son; and he called his name Jesus.'

One cannot conclude from this text that Mary had sexual intercourse with Joseph after the birth of Jesus. Matthew's intention is to emphasize that Mary was virgin when Jesus was born.

The expression 'until' marks the vigour of this assertion. It is used frequently in the Bible: 'Sit at my right hand until I make your enemies your footstool' (Ps. 110). We do not conclude from this that Christ will not sit at God's right hand after his enemies have been vanquished. Here is another example: 'No one knows his (Moses') tomb until this day' (Deut. 34.6). We do not deduce from this that according to scripture one day it will have to be rediscovered.

We use the same expression nowadays. A mother may say to her children, 'be good until I get back.' That hardly means that they are to be naughty when she does get back. Rather, the phrase is meant to make a remark emphatic.

Virginal and spiritual motherhood in respect of men and women

It is inconceivable that Mary should have renounced her virginity after God had sanctified it by giving birth.

On the other hand, if Jesus is from all eternity the only Son of the Father, he should also, in time, have been the one son of Mary.

It would not be fitting for Mary's womb, sanctified by the Holy Spirit, to serve for the conception and bearing of others who would necessarily have been sinners.

In that case Christ would have had brothers of a specific fleshly kind. But he came into this world to be the brother of all men, the universal brother, and to found a brotherhood according to the Spirit.

The new Israel 'according to the Spirit'

The new Israel is no longer the people of God to whom one belongs by the ties of flesh and blood, but a people of God according to the Spirit. One belongs to this people by the new baptismal birth of water and the Spirit.

That is why Jesus was not to marry. In him were to be realized the spiritual nuptials between God and humankind, and this would exclude Jesus being able to engender human descendants who would have been a Christian people after the flesh.

So as mother of Christ, Mary too was to dedicate herself wholly to this new people of God, that of the new covenant.

Mary, mother of the Church

Mother of Christ the head, she was to dedicate herself to all those who were called to become the members of the ecclesial body of Jesus.

At the time of the incarnation, in becoming mother of Christ, Mary became mother of the Church. This spiritual motherhood with regard to all humankind, like her physical motherhood with regard to the Son of God, excludes any other biological motherhood than that of Jesus.

Mary is *mater socia*, the mother associated with the Redeemer, the mother of the Redeemer as

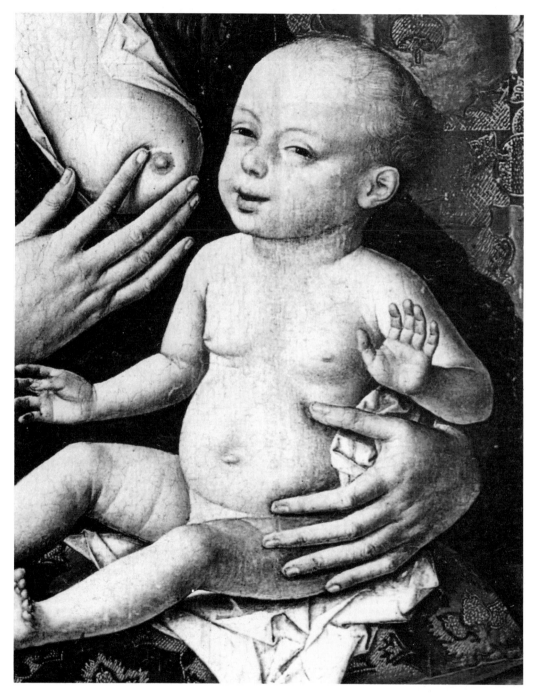

Virgin and Child. Thierry Bouts. The National Gallery, London.

Redeemer. This association with Christ the Saviour, with his mission of universal salvation, required of Mary a total dedication to the saving mission of Jesus and to his person.

If there is one human person who in the Church should have been virgin in order to devote themselves totally to Christ and his work, it is Mary as mother of Christ and mother of humankind.

Mary was to be the first of the consecrated virgins. A mother who bears a son who is the Son of God can and should give herself, devote herself without reserve to her child, love him in a total and absolute way.

This behaviour would be abnormal in the case of an ordinary birth. A child, no matter what his importance, is not everything for the mother who bears him. He is the basis of a new love of his mother for her husband and calls, if that is possible, for the birth of other children.

Certainly there are women who marry only to have a child or for whom the husband counts less once they have a child. This behaviour is regrettable. The love of a mother for her child must not be idolatrous. But when this child is God, he must be everything for the woman who gives birth to him.

Mary and Joseph understood that they had to dedicate themselves to their child, who had been sent by God, and to his divine mission. There was nothing egotistic about their virginity in marriage; on the contrary, it was openness, pure receptivity to the gift of God, for the salvation of all humankind.

Mary's virginal motherhood takes on meaning in relationship to Christ, but also in relation to all of us, in relation to all the church.

According to the flesh Mary was not to have a child other than Jesus so that she could become the spiritual mother of us all, the mother of the whole Church.

So for us Mary will always remain the 'Holy Virgin'. Her virginity and her motherhood are inseparable, since her motherhood is essentially virginal. Mary is not a mother though virgin, but she is virgin because she is mother of Christ and of all humankind.

The Virgin. Russian icon.

The Virgin Mary, model for virgins

From the fourth century the Fathers, and especially St Athanasisus and St Ambrose, celebrated the virginity of Mary to exalt Christian virginity in the Church. Conversely, those who challenge the virginity of Mary put in question the value of the state of virginity in the Church.

As 'queen of virgins', Mary is their perfect model. As we read in the German catechism for adults, in history this truth of faith has helped Christians to understand the meaning of the ideal of freely chosen celibacy.

Vatican II proclaims: 'The mother of God is a type of the Church in the order of faith, charity and perfect union with Christ. For in the mystery of the Church, which is itself rightly called mother and virgin, the Blessed Virgin stands out in eminent and singular fashion as exemplar both of virgin and mother' (*Lumen Gentium*, 63).

The Virgin Mary, a model of availability for all Christians

For all Christians, even for those who are not called to dedicated celibacy, the virginity of Mary is an exhortation to complete availability, for all Christians are called to holiness (*Lumen Gentium*, ch. V, on the universal call to holiness in the church).

However, we must neither oppose nor separate Christian virginity and Christian marriage. In the Church, the sacrament of marriage and dedicated celibacy cannot be understood without each other. The one confirms the other.

Christian marriage is a sacrament because it is a sign of the union of Christ and the Church. And as such it is also an effective cause of sanctifying grace. This union of Christ and the Church was first realized in Mary when she said 'yes' to the spiritual nuptials of Christ and the Church.

So Christian spouses may find in the virginal 'yes' of Mary, that of both mother and bride, a model of consent to their conjugal union. Their accord is sealed with the sign of this union of Christ and the Church, which was first realized in Mary.

They should welcome the grace of their union and partake in the sacrament of marriage with the same availability as Mary when she welcomed the Saviour.

So by her virginity, for all Christians in the Church Mary is the model of pure receptivity of free grace from above, the model of free acceptance, by faith and love, of the grace of salvation.

3
Mary's Holiness

This chapter falls into two sections. In the first, we shall see that Mary was exempt from original sin and that she received divine grace at the time of her conception.

In the second, I shall show how her holiness progressed throughout her earthly life before attaining its fullness in the glory of heavenly life.

The Immaculate Conception

Mary was preserved from original sin from the first moment of her existence. That defines the privilege of the Immaculate Conception.

The significance of the Immaculate Conception

First of all we must correct a serious misunderstanding. For many people the Immaculate Conception is about the active conception of Jesus by Mary. In that case the Immaculate Conception would denote the fact that Mary had conceived Christ without her motherhood being tainted with sin.

This interpretation is bound up with the aberrant idea that all human motherhood is tainted and that all sexual acts, even in the holiest marriage, are contaminated with sin.

Preservation from original sin

In truth, the Immaculate Conception is about the fact that Mary was conceived in the womb of her mother, St Anne, without contracting original sin as we all do.

This is not sin in the strict sense, like all the sins that we are personally responsible for committing. In an analogous sense, the state of original sin at birth signifies that our native condition is not of itself compatible with friendship with God or effective participation in God's divine life. This participation is conferred, after birth, by filial rebirth in Jesus Christ, brought about by the sacrament of baptism or what is supplied by that sacrament.

The doctrine of original sin at least affirms that all human beings at birth come into the world affected by original sin by reason of the sin of Adam, in other words through solidarity with humanity which has universally and in solidarity been sinful from the beginning.

So original sin, at birth, is not a kind of stain which is removed by baptism. It is a deprivation of the sanctifying grace effectively given to the child by baptism.

To say that Mary was preserved from original sin from her conception onwards is thus to make the positive statement that from the first moment of her existence she was sanctified by the grace of the divine life which is given to others only after their birth.

By reason of her future divine motherhood Mary was given divine grace at the time of her conception; this grace anticipated baptismal grace.

The privilege of a preventive redemption

This is a privilege, since it is a definition of faith that Mary, unlike other infants, was preserved from original sin 'by the singular grace and privilege of the omnipotent God' (*Ineffabilis Deus*).

However, Mary, too, belongs to our ransomed humanity. So it is a virtue of the redemption brought about by Christ, the sole saviour of all, that like all humankind she was able to receive sanctifying grace. For Mary as for all her human brothers and sisters, this was a redemptive grace from Christ.

Mary was redeemed, but in a preventive way. The other members of the human community first of all contract original sin and grow without the grace of the divine life, and only receive it later. Mary did not contract original sin; God kept it from her. Like us, she was redeemed by virtue of the merits of Christ, but her redemption was preservative whereas ours is reparative.

Redeemed in the best way

Theologians say that Mary was redeemed *meliori modo*, 'in the best way'.

Vatican II explains this point: 'Redeemed in a more exalted fashion, by reason of the merits of her son and united to him by a close and indissoluble tie, she is endowed with the high office and dignity of the Mother of the Son of God, and therefore she is also the beloved daughter of the Father and the temple of the Holy Spirit. Because of this gift of sublime grace she far surpasses all creatures, both in heaven and on earth' (*Lumen Gentium*, 53).

Later on, Vatican II speaks of the 'Immaculate Virgin preserved free from all stain of original sin' (*Lumen Gentium*, 59; read also *Redemptoris Mater*, 10).

The feast of 8 December

In its prayers, the Feast of the Immaculate Conception, on 8 December, invites us to meditate on this favour by which God prepared in Mary a worthy dwelling for her son, filling her with grace. This grace was absolutely free, as is all grace of vocation or sanctification which predestines us to salvation.

In the Letter to the Ephesians, read at this festival, St Paul says that God chose us before the creation of the world and that he has destined us in advance to become his children through Jesus Christ (1.4–5).

It is our vocation to become children of the God who predestined the Son of God to become incarnate in Mary and to be penetrated at the time of his conception with the grace of God.

Mary's predestination

This predestination was underlined by Pius IX in the constitution *Ineffabilis Deus* for the definition of the Immaculate Conception (8 December 1854). Mary was endowed with a grace distinct from ours since, unlike us, she received it at the time of her conception. But this is the same grace of divine life accorded to all Christians on the day of their baptism.

This exceptional situation makes Mary the first member of redeemed humanity, the type of the Church of the redeemed.

The Virgin. El Greco.
Museum of Fine Arts, Strasbourg.

The progressive development of the dogma of the Immaculate Conception

It took time for the Church to become progressively aware of this privilege reserved for Mary by reason of her motherhood. We do not find any explicit evidence for it in scripture, even if, as we shall see, it is implicitly contained in the revealed mystery of the divine motherhood. That is why in defining the Immaculate Conception as a dogma of faith, Pius IX did not base his definition on biblical statements but on the universal faith of the church.

> We declare, pronounce and define that the Most Blessed Virgin Mary, at the first instant of her Conception was preserved immaculate from all stain of original sin, by the singular grace and privilege of the Omnipotent God, in virtue of the merits of Jesus Christ, the Saviour of mankind, and that this doctrine was revealed by God, and therefore, must be believed firmly and constantly by all the faithful.
>
> The Infallible Definition, *Ineffabilis Deus*

The preparation of the definition

This definition was preceded by a long preparation. Pius IX consulted theologians chosen as experts and entrusted the preparatory work to a congregation of cardinals.

Pius IX had already been instructed by the feelings of numerous bishops who called on him to define the dogma of the Immaculate Conception. These episcopal requests for a definition go back as far as the beginning of the fifteenth century. In the nineteenth century, the demonstrations connected with the miraculous medal of the rue du Bac in Paris in 1830 (see below) and the conversion of Alphonse Ratisbonne in 1842 had contributed towards prompting new petitions; these increased under the pontificate of Gregory XVI.

However, Pius IX wanted to consult all the bishops of the Catholic Church. He sent an encyclical to all of them dated Gaeta, 2 February 1849. In it he asked them to make known to him in writing what were the faith and piety of those in their care concerning the Immaculate Conception of Mary. And above all he asked them what they thought and what they wanted in connection with the project of the definition.

Of the 600 bishops consulted, 546 pronounced themselves explicitly in favour of the definition. The others were opposed, above all for opportunistic reasons. Only four or five bishops thought that the Immaculate Conception could not be defined as a divinely revealed truth.

Starting from the current faith of the Church to return to its source

So we shall start from this universal faith, defined in 1854, to retrace the course of a long Church tradition. This course will take us back to Holy Scripture, in which the church, in a progressive development of awareness, has been able to discern the embryo of the Immaculate Conception, in an implicit way, in the deposit of revelation.

We shall return from the current doctrine defined by the Church to its source, in the same way as one can go up from the mouth of a river which had become broad and deep, to discover the tiny spring which is its source.

Pontifical decrees of the seventeenth century

Well before Pius IX's definition, in the seventeenth century, a number of pontifical decrees had approved and recommended the teaching of the doctrine of the Immaculate Conception. They had even forbidden the public statement of the contrary opinion, on pain of ecclesiastical sanctions.

Alexander VII in 1661, Gregory XV in 1622 and Paul V in 1617 pronounced in favour of this belief. As Pius IX observed in the constitution *Ineffabilis Deus*, they had written clearly and manifestly that the conception of the Virgin was the feast that was being celebrated, and they proscribed as false and quite alien to the thought of the church the opinion of those who believed and affirmed that it was not the immaculate conception but the sanctification (after conception) of the Holy Virgin which the Church honoured. (John the Baptist, for example, was sanctified before his birth but not at the moment of his conception.)

Pius IX also attacked those who imagined a distinction between the first and second instant of conception and claimed that the truth was that what was being celebrated was not the conception but the first moment after conception. This was because, in order to safeguard the principle of the redemption of all human beings by Christ, some imagined that there was a first moment when Mary had been conceived with original sin and a second instant immediately afterwards when she had been sanctified. This was the sense in which they thought it possible to preach and celebrate the Immaculate Conception. But in reality this was to deny the Immaculate Conception as the Church understands it, since Mary never knew original sin.

St Pius V, in 1567

In 1567, St Pius V condemned the proposition of Baius that no one apart from Christ had been exempted from original sin and that the death and tribulations of Mary had been a penalty for actual sins or for original sin.

The Council of Trent

The Council of Trent inserted into its decree on original sin (in 1546 and 1547) the important declaration that in the decree relating to original sin it had no intention of including the blessed and immaculate Virgin Mary, mother of God, but that it was necessary to observe the constitutions of Pope Sixtus IV, under the threat of the penalties which these constitutions contained and which Trent renewed.

Sixtus IV, in 1483

In 1483 Sixtus IV had in effect approved the new office and new mass of the Immaculate Conception and forbade the parties in conflict over the subject of the doctrine of the Immaculate Conception to censure each other.

As early as 1439 the Council of Basle had expressed its support for the doctrine of the Immaculate Conception.

The feast of the Immaculate Conception, which became a feast of obligation in 1708 and which had already taken root almost universally by the fourteenth century, in fact goes back to the seventh century in the East, where the feast of the conception of Mary was celebrated.

The mediaeval controversies

However, during the Middle Ages, supporters and opponents of the Immaculate Conception came into conflict: great saints and great theologians clashed over the subject.

We should not be surprised at these disagreements. Here again, as in the case of the divine motherhood, the development of marian doctrine was bound up with the development of other Christian truths.

As long as the doctrine of original sin in us had remained obscure, the problem of the Immaculate Conception of Mary could neither be raised nor resolved in formal terms.

It should be no surprise that when the question was posed sharply in the Middle Ages, St Bernard, a fervent marian doctor, was opposed to the introduction of the feast of the Immaculate Conception, 8 December, and St Thomas Aquinas rejected the doctrine, out of a concern to safeguard the universality of redemption. In fact the problem was how the Immaculate Conception could be reconciled with the affirmation that Mary was really redeemed like all of us by Jesus Christ, the unique saviour of humankind.

Duns Scotus (who died in 1308) has the credit of having found the answer which was to be taken up in the dogmatic definition. The redemptive action of Christ is extended to Mary by anticipation, in order to preserve her from original sin. Mary was indeed redeemed, but *meliori modo*, in a better and preventive way. According to Scotus, preservation from original sin is the most perfect form of redemption. So it was fitting that Christ should have redeemed his mother in this way.

The Franciscan order adopted Scotus' view

41

The Virgin in Glory. Painted altar front. Catalan. Twelfth century.

and resolutely supported the doctrine and feast of the Immaculate Conception of Mary against the Dominican order.

But let us continue to go back through the past to the patristic age.

The affirmations of the Fathers

The Church Fathers did not affirm the Immaculate Conception in explicit terms. But they did emphasize Mary's holiness, perfect and without restriction.

> Hence the Fathers have never ceased to call the Mother of God the lily among thorns, or the earth entirely intact, virginal, undefiled, immaculate, ever-blessed and free from all corruption of sin, from which was formed the New Adam; or the flawless, brightest and most pleasant paradise of innocence, immortality and delights planted by God Himself and protected against all snare of the poisonous Serpent; or the incorruptible wood the worm of sin had never corrupted; or the fountain ever clear and sealed by the power of the Holy Spirit; or the most divine temple; or the treasure of immortality; or the one and only daughter not of death but of life, the child not of anger but of grace, which by the singular providence of God has always blossomed, though it sprang from a corrupt and infected root, contrary to the ordinary and fixed laws.
>
> *Ineffabilis Deus*, I, 1

In the fourth century, in praying to Christ St Ephraem said: 'You and your mother are the only ones who are entirely beautiful *in every respect*, for in you, O Lord, there is no spot, and in your mother there is no stain' (*Carmina nisibena*, XXVII).

St Augustine (who died in 430) excluded Mary from general culpability, but without specifying the absence of original sin; he speaks explicitly of the absence of personal sins: 'With the exception of the Virgin Mary, of whom I want there to be no question when one talks of sin – for the sake of

the Lord's honour. We know that she received superabundant grace to win an absolute victory over sin from the fact that she had the merit to conceive and bear him who was incontestably without sin' (*On the nature of grace*, XLVI).

At the beginning of the third century St Hippolytus had compared Mary with an incorruptible tree that no worm could gnaw at.

The theme of the New Eve

In the second century, St Justin and St Irenaeus exalted Mary's holiness, showing that she is the New Eve and that she made good Eve's disobedience by her own obedience. Since I have already quoted St Irenaeus in the first chapter, here I shall cite St Justin.

> We understand that he became man by the Virgin in order that the disobedience which proceeded from the serpent might receive its destruction in the same manner in which it derived its origin. For Eve, who was a virgin and undefiled, having conceived the word of the serpent, brought full disobedience and death. But the Virgin Mary received faith and joy when the angel Gabriel announced the good tidings to her that the spirit of the Lord would come upon her and the power of the Highest would overshadow her; wherefore also the Holy Thing begotten of her is the Son of God; and she replied, 'Be it unto me according to thy word.' But by her has He been born to whom so many scriptures refer, and by whom God destroys both the serpent and those angels and men who are like him, but brings deliverance from death to those who repent of their wickedness and believe in him.
>
> Justin, *Dialogue with Trypho*, ch. 100

Now when the Fathers developed this theme of Mary, the new Eve, and exalted Mary as the ideal of virtue, they did so by commenting on both the text of the annunciation (Luke 1.26–38) and that of the protevangelium (Gen. 3.9–20).

Through this patristic theme on Mary, the New Eve, we attain as it were the scriptural source of the traditional doctrine of the Immaculate Conception which was to be developed into a doctrinal formulation by Pius IX.

The mass of the Feast of the Immaculate Conception has the text of the protevangelium as the first reading and that of the annunciation as the third reading.

If we read these two texts of scripture independently of their patristic interpretation, without taking account of the living tradition of the church, we cannot find in them explicit testimony to the Immaculate Conception. Furthermore, the dogmatic constitution of Pius IX presents them as testimonies of the patristic tradition and not as strict scriptural proofs.

However, if we go in depth into these texts on which the Church has meditated over the centuries, we can discover that the Immaculate Conception is implicitly contained in them. Here we must not interpret them as specific texts taken in isolation but put them in the context of all the biblical evidence about Mary and her role in the history of salvation.

The annunciation to Mary (Luke 1.26–38)

The angel hailed Mary, saying to her, 'Rejoice, for you have found favour with God, the Lord is with you' (Luke 1.28). We take up this salutation in the *Ave Maria*, 'Hail Mary, full of grace', recognizing in Mary a fullness of sanctifying grace.

kecharitōmenē does not refer literally to the fullness of sanctifying grace given to Mary at the time of her conception, but to the favour done to her of being mother of the Lord, as we have already seen. However, the personal holiness of Mary is certainly implied in this term which is presented as a proper name given to Mary, as being inherent in the very grace of her motherhood.

When God calls a person to become an instrument of his saving plan, God does not make use of him or her as a simple physical instrument – here, in the case of Mary, as a simple instrument of biological generation; God appeals to the free co-operation of her faith, penetrating her with a grace of faith and love which is a grace of divine life inherent in the soul that gives it interior grace.

So the grace of motherhood implies in Mary a state of supernatural grace which makes her fully worthy to receive the Saviour in her womb.

The Holy Spirit was to come upon Mary and the power of the Most High was to overshadow her (Luke 1.35), so that the Son of God should be conceived in her womb.

Must not this same Holy Spirit also have filled Mary in her soul with a sanctifying grace of divine life which made her the purest tabernacle of the divine Saviour and capable of loving her son with a human motherly love profoundly steeped in divine love?

Better still, for this motherly love of Mary's to be completely pure and holy at the moment of the incarnation, was it not fitting that at the time

---

It is no wonder that it was customary for the Fathers to refer to the Mother of God as all holy and free from every stain of sin, as though fashioned by the Holy Spirit and formed as a new creature. Enriched from the first instant of her conception with the splendour of an entirely unique holiness, the virgin of Nazareth is hailed by the heralding angel, by divine command, as 'full of grace' (cf. Luke 1.28).

Lumen Gentium, 56

of her conception Mary should have been preserved from all sin and sanctified by the gift of the grace of divine life which is the personal gift of the Holy Spirit?

This interpretation of the salutation of the angel at the moment of the annunciation, which recognizes Mary as being 'full of grace', thus has a legitimate foundation in the mystery of Mary's motherhood as this has been understood by the Church in its progressive awareness of revelation.

This ecclesial interpretation was taken up by Vatican II (*Lumen Gentium*, 56) and by John Paul II (*Redemptoris Mater*, 8 and 9).

The protevangelium (Gen. 3.15)

Messianic interpretation

'The Lord God said to the serpent, "I will put enmity between you and the woman, between your seed and her seed; this shall bruise your head, and you shall bruise his heel."'

The pronoun 'this' denotes the posterity of the woman, i.e. all the offspring of the good who one day will be victorious over the offspring of the serpent, a symbol of Satan and the race of the devil. It is the offspring, the 'seed' of the woman who will be victorious.

But we know that the good will only be able to conquer Satan and his sinful empire through Christ the Redeemer, who himself will be among the offspring of the women and will come 'to destroy the works of the devil' (I John 3.8).

According to the literal sense of the text, the offspring of the woman includes Christ the Redeemer and *par excellence* denotes him personally.

This is doubtless the reason why the Greek translation used the masculine *autos* to denote the 'seed' (the offspring) of the woman, in place of the neuter required by 'seed'.

The protevangelium is certainly messianic. But like all the prophecies, it is still very vague in its indications. It announces in an imprecise way a victory of the good over the evil. This is a general promise of salvation which only becomes meaningful when it is realized in Jesus.

Marian interpretation

Many theologians, heirs of patristic exegesis, have also interpreted the protevangelium in a marian sense which reinforces its messianic sense.

The woman whose descendants denote Christ *par excellence* would herself, *par excellence*, denote the Virgin Mary, mother of the Redeemer. There is no question of retaining the Latin translation of the Vulgate, which has replaced the masculine pronoun *ipse* by the feminine, *ipsa*, to indicate that Mary is the one who bruises the serpent's head. It is the *semen*, the seed, of the woman, her offspring, in other words Christ, and not the woman herself who will bruise the serpent's head.

Now does not the woman whose descendants will conquer those of the serpent *par excellence* denote the Virgin Mary herself?

If one accepts this point, then perhaps according to the marian interpretation also adopted by the Fathers one can recognize that the prophecy of the protevangelium does not relate only to Eve, the first woman, mother of all living beings, but also to the Virgin Mary, the New Eve, mother of Christ the Saviour.

According to this marian interpretation the protevangelium would announce that in giving birth to Christ the Redeemer the Virgin Mary won a decisive victory over evil. But would this victory over evil have been total had Mary, if only for an instant, been in the grips of evil, in the grips of Satan represented by the serpent tempter? That is what led to the conclusion from the promise of the protevangelium that Mary the New Eve, victorious over the descendants of the serpent, must have been preserved from any taint of evil, not only from any personal sin but also from original sin itself.

So Vatican II affirmed: 'Considered in this light, she is already prophetically foreshadowed in the promise of victory over the serpent which was given to our first parents after their fall into sin' (*Lumen Gentium*, 55).

Virgin of the Apocalypse.
Detail of the tapestry of the Apocalypse. Angers. Fourteenth century.

Mary's motherhood, the basic reason for her Immaculate Conception

This primordial reason was brought out by Pius IX at the beginning of the constitution *Ineffabilis Deus*. I have already emphasized this in the interpretation of the story of the annunciation, so we shall not return to it at length here.

Mary, mother of God, could not have the least complicity with sin. The one who finds herself so close to God must be completely pure and holy, since we know that the divine love sanctifies human beings who do not put obstacles in its way, the moment it reaches them. That is all the more reason why the Son of God made man, carried nine months by Mary, should have sanctified the one in whom he lay. Surely he must already have prepared the Virgin Mary to become his purest tabernacle from the first moment of her existence?

The motherly love of Mary for her son Jesus was and is a love of God, since it was a love of the Son of God made man.

Now if it is true that no perfect love of God is possible for a human creature without a sanctifying grace of divine love, how can Mary have truly been able to love Jesus without her human motherly love being divinely made supernatural through sanctifying grace? And so if Mary was to love the Son of God with such pure love the moment she became a mother, must she not have received this grace of divine love at the moment of her conception, in such a way that sin was never able to deprive her of this supernatural capacity for divine love?

Mary's Perpetual and Progressive Holiness

Mary, all her life preserved from all sin

Exempt from all personal faults, Mary was, as the Eastern Church says, 'all holy'. The testimonies invoked for the Immaculate Conception apply equally to affirming the absence in Mary of any personal sin.

An undefined truth of faith

This truth has never been the specific object of a dogmatic definition. However, it is part of the universal tradition of the Church.

The conviction that Mary did not commit any personal sin was received very early in the Church, well before there was any awareness of her exemption from original sin.

Without doubt some Greek Fathers – Origen, John Chrysostom and Cyril of Alexandria – accepted that Mary could have known some shortcomings of vanity at the time of the miracle of Cana, or of faith, at the foot of the cross. In contrast, the Latin Fathers resolutely argued for the absence of all sin in Mary. And St Thomas Aquinas, who did not accept the Immaculate

Our Lady. Detail of stained-glass window. Cathedral of Chartres. Twelfth century.

48

Conception, affirmed without beating about the bush: 'The blessed Virgin Mary received such full intensity of grace that it brought her right next to the author of grace in order to receive him, who had full intensity of grace, into herself' (*Summa Theologica* III, 27.5 ad 2).

This exemption of Mary from all sin was mentioned by the Council of Trent when it defined the impossibility of anyone living here on earth without any sin, even venial: 'If anyone says that a man once justified can no longer sin nor lose grace and thus that anyone who falls and sins has never been really justified, or on the contrary that during his life he can avoid all sin, even venial sin, except by a special privilege of God, as the Church holds in the case of the blessed Virgin, let him be anathema.'

So this is an assured doctrine, and one could even call it an undefined truth of faith.

Mary, ever virgin

Pius XII in his encyclical of 1943 on the mystical body (*Mystici Corporis Christi*) says that Mary was 'free from all sin, original and personal'. No human being, even the holiest, can avoid all venial sin throughout his or her life. But Mary, by virtue of a particular grace of impeccability, was confirmed in grace, established in the love of charity, to the point of never being able to sin.

This absence of all sin does not imply that Mary performed an uninterrupted series of extraordinary or heroic actions of a spectacular and marvellous kind. She expressed this by a holiness which was at the same time both total and quite simple. This holiness of Mary 'the all holy' was the consequence and the extension of the grace of her Immaculate Conception.

From the start wholly placed under the guidance of the Holy Spirit, she was able to lead her life and develop without any infidelity, in friendship with God and participating in God's life, under the sign of the perfect New Covenant with him.

Certainly, at first sight, such an affirmation

The Virgin. St Clement of Taull, Spain. 1123.

might surprise us. Are not human beings sinners? Are we not by nature feeble, fragile, sinful, and do we not become sinners at the age of discretion?

Do not all human beings, in their human truthfulness, recognize that they are sinners before abandoning themselves totally to God's mercy? And do they not do this counting on the salvation which comes from a forgiveness which is obtained through the merits of Christ, the sole redeemer?

Mary, always redeemed

This new question about the exemption of Mary from all personal sin produces the same answer as the question of the Immaculate Conception.

49

In order not to sin personally, Mary needed a continual gift of graces. These graces, like those of the Immaculate Conception, were the redemptive graces of Christ. Redeemed *Meliori modo* at the moment of her conception, throughout her life she was continually redeemed 'in the best way', being graced with redemptive graces which made her capable of not failing.

Mary, 'the all holy', never ceased to be the 'wholly redeemed'.

Progressive sanctification in the course of a life of trials undergone in the 'obedience of faith'

The privilege of the grace given to Mary does not have any implications, the absence of sin apart, that would remove her from the common human situation.

The experience of the life of the saints shows that if they received more graces than others, they were predestined to undergo more trials, overcome more sufferings, encounter more crosses, on a road which led many of them to martyrdom.

'If any man would come after me, let him deny himself and take up his cross daily and follow me. For whoever would save his life will lose it; and whoever loses his life for my sake, he will save it' (Luke 9.23–24). No Christian followed this directive of Jesus better than his own mother.

Progressive sanctification

It was indeed a privilege that incomparable grace was given to Mary at the beginning of her existence. But in Mary, the power of the divine strength was put at the service of an enhanced generosity and a constant effort. Every trial undergone in the obedience of faith was for her the occasion of a new surpassing of herself in the way of a holiness which reached its fulfilment only on the day of her glorious assumption.

'The obedience of faith'

In his encyclical, John Paul II has retraced this way of Mary, presenting it as a pilgrimage of faith that the Church must undertake in its turn, following her example.

St Paul often speaks in his letters of the 'obedience of faith' by which human beings commit themselves wholly, submitting freely to the word and will of God who reveals himself to them (Rom. 1.5; 16.26).

According to the testimony of the Gospels, this obedience of faith characterizes the holiness of Mary throughout her earthly life in which, contrary to what some mariologists have said, she did not enjoy a grace of the beatific vision.

At the annunciation

John Paul II writes: 'At the annunciation, Mary entrusted herself entirely to God . . . manifesting the "obedience of faith"' (*Redemptoris Mater*, 13). She uttered her 'yes' in faith, without knowing the future unfolding of her mission as mother.

The presentation of Jesus in the Temple

'Later, a little further along this way of "the obedience of faith" Mary hears other words: those uttered by Simeon in the Temple of Jerusalem' (*Redemptoris Mater*, 16). 'Behold, this child is set for the fall and rising of many in Israel, and for a sign that is spoken against, that thoughts out of many hearts may be revealed.' And Simeon adds, speaking directly to Mary, 'And a sword will pierce through your own soul also' (Luke 2.34–35).

John Paul II writes: 'Simeon's words seem like a *second* Annunciation to Mary, for they tell her of the actual historical situation in which the Son is to accomplish his mission, namely in misunderstanding and sorrow. While this announcement on the one hand confirms her faith in the accomplishment of the divine promises of salvation, on the other hand it also reveals to her that she will have to live her obedience of faith in suffering, at the side of the suffering Saviour, and that her motherhood will be mysterious and sorrowful' (*Redemptoris Mater*, 16; the prophecy of Simeon is recalled in *Lumen Gentium*, 57).

The hidden life at Nazareth

After the death of Herod there begins the long period of Jesus' hidden life, in Nazareth.

'She "who believed that there would be a fulfilment of what was spoken to her from the Lord" (Luke 1.45) lives the reality of these words day by day' (*Redemptoris Mater*, 17).

During the years of Jesus' hidden life in his home at Nazareth, the life of Mary is also 'hidden with Christ in God' (Col. 3.3). Every day, Mary is in the presence of the mystery of God made man, a mystery which surpasses all that was revealed in the old covenant.

However, Mary is in contact with the truth of her son only in faith and by faith. Mary has no direct vision of God. She sees a human child, doubtless recognized as sent by God, but her motherly relationship with Jesus is psychologically the same as that of any mother to her child, with the same emotional reactions and the same human behaviour.

Jesus lost in the temple

This relationship appears clearly when Jesus at the age of twelve remains among the doctors in the temple, letting Mary and Joseph return without him. Mary's reaction is that of any mother: '"Son, why have you treated us so? Behold, your father and I have been looking for you anxiously?" And he said to them, "How is it that you sought me? Did you not know that I must be in my Father's house?" And they did not understand the saying that he spoke to them' (Luke 2.48–50). 'And Mary kept all these things in her heart' (Luke 2.51).

Mary had to progress in faith in order to discern the mystery of the divine Sonship of her son, which doubtless she recognized fully only with the light of the Holy Spirit given at Pentecost. And she was not to see God face to face in the divine person of her Son until the day of her glorious assumption.

The 'dark night' of the mystics

Before arriving at this heavenly vision, she had to believe in faith, with pain in her heart, undergoing a kind of 'dark night of the soul', to use St John of the Cross's expression, as a 'veil' under which she had to approach the invisible and live in the intimacy of the mystery. This is

---

When the child Jesus was lost and they had sought him sorrowing, his parents found him in the temple, engaged in the things that were his Father's, and they did not understand the words of their Son. His mother, however, kept all these things to be pondered in her heart (cf. Luke 2.41–51).

Lumen Gentium, 57

how for many years Mary remained in the intimacy of the mystery of her son and advanced on her way of faith, while Jesus 'grew in wisdom and grace before God and man' (Luke 2.52).

'Blessed is she who believed'

So day by day there was fulfilled in Mary the blessing uttered by Elizabeth at the Visitation: 'Blessed is she who believed' (Luke 1.45; *Redemptoris Mater*, 17).

This blessing attains its fullness of meaning when Mary stands at the foot of the cross (John 19.25). It took much faith for Mary to be able to sustain a mystery as disconcerting as that of the crucifixion.

So Mary's holiness found its fulfilment only at the end of an earthly pilgrimage, a true way of the cross which she experienced in faith.

Mary, the holiest member of the church

In his encyclical on the mystical body, Pius XII writes: 'May the Virgin Mother of God hear our prayers – she whose sinless soul was filled with the divine Spirit of Jesus Christ above all other created souls.'

Vatican II said of Mary: 'She is the beloved daughter of the Father and the temple of the Holy Spirit. Because of this gift of sublime grace she far surpasses all creatures, both in heaven and on earth' (*Lumen Gentium*, 53, a text quoted in *Redemptoris Mater*, 9).

And again: 'Mary has by grace been exalted above all angels and men to a place second only to her Son, as the most holy mother of God who was involved in the mysteries of Christ: she is rightly honoured by a special cult in the Church' (*Lumen Gentium*, 66).

Do we have to be more specific? Theologians or spiritual writers have spent a good deal of time on this subject, asking what was the degree of Mary's grace on her last day, and what was her degree of holiness in relationship to that of all the other saints. However, let us leave these writers and men of prayer to their subtle research.

At that moment (of the annunciation) she had also heard the words: 'He will be great . . . and the Lord God will give to him the throne of his father David, and he will reign over the house of Jacob for ever; and of his kingdom there will be no end' (Luke 1.32–33).

And now, standing at the foot of the Cross, Mary is the witness, humanly speaking, of the complete negation of these words. On that wood of the Cross her Son hangs in agony as one condemned. 'He was despised and rejected by men; a man of sorrows . . . he was despised, and we esteemed him not': as one destroyed (cf. Isa. 53.3–5). How great, how heroic then is the obedience of faith shown by Mary in the face of God's 'unsearchable judgments'! How completely she 'abandons herself to God' without reserve, 'offering the full assent of the intellect and the will' to him whose 'ways are inscrutable' (cf. Rom 11.33)! And how powerful too is the action of grace in her soul, how all-pervading is the influence of the Holy Spirit and of his light and power!

Redemptoris Mater, 18

The Virgin. Detail, Polyptych of the Last Judgment.
Rogier Van der Weyden. Hotel-Dieu, Beaune.

The human person who is most united to God

Let us remember what is certainly inherent in the mystery of her divine motherhood: Mary, among the saints, is the member of the Church who came closest to the holiness of Jesus. The holiness of a human creature is measured by his or her degree of union with God.

As mother of Christ, Son of God, Mary was the human person who was most united with God and was most closely associated with the redemptive mission of the incarnate Word. Intimately united with Christ by her motherhood, through her life Mary lived up to the mother's mission which was hers in the history of salvation.

Rather than measure Mary's holiness quantitatively, let us see how Mary qualitatively represents both the most perfect and the simplest Christian holiness.

The most total and the simplest holiness

The other saints developed something of the holiness of Jesus by imitating one or other of his virtues more specifically.

St Francis of Assisi specially imitated Christ in his poverty. St Dominic above all followed his love of truth. St Ignatius Loyola wanted to follow Jesus in the mystery of his filial obedience to the Father.

The holiness of Christ is of such richness that it takes a multitude of saints to reflect the diversity of its many aspects.

From this point of view the holiness of those who have imitated Christ has some particular aspect by which each differs from the other.

But Mary is distinct from all the other saints because she imitated the holiness of her son in the most absolute and the simplest way.

Mary is the Christian *par excellence* who has left us the example of trust, a synthesis of the three theological virtues of faith, hope and love, living out quite simply this abandonment in the everyday existence of an apparently quite ordinary life.

Mary did not accomplish anything spectacular or exceptional to attract the attention of the world. She went unseen. She played no role like that of the apostles, whether in the evangelization of the world or the organization of the church. Moreover, it took time even in the church for the greatness of her divine motherhood to be recognized fully.

Distance was required to see in the life of Mary all the grace and glory of God that she received.

Mary, model of holiness

That is why the holiness of Mary in its simplest and most ordinary realization is also the holiness that is most accessible and the most possible to imitate.

If we are to consider Mary, the refuge of sinners, we must certainly affirm that on earth she was the only one to be exempt from sin.

However, her poor, modest and discreet existence offers us poor sinners a model of holiness at the heart of everyday existence that we are able to imitate. Her life, the most ordinary possible, was finally revealed as the holiest possible.

St Thérèse of Lisieux understood that very well.

How I would have liked to be a priest so that I could preach about the Virgin Mary! I think that once would have been enough to express my thoughts on this matter.

First I would have shown how little is known of the life of the Holy Virgin. It would not be necessary to say improbable things about her or whatever: for example, that when she was quite small, at the age of three, she went to the Temple to offer herself to God with ardent sentiments of love and an extraordinary fervour, when perhaps she went quite simply in obedience to her parents . . .

And why say again, in connection with the prophetic words of the old man Simeon, that from that moment the Holy Virgin had the passion of Jesus constantly before her eyes . . .

If a sermon on the Holy Virgin is to bear fruit, it must show her real life as the Gospel makes us see it, and not her supposed life; and we can guess that her real life, at Nazareth and later, must have been quite ordinary.

The Holy Virgin is portrayed as being inapproachable; but she would be depicted as someone we can imitate, practising hidden virtues. It should be said that she lived by faith, as we do, with evidence for this drawn from the gospel, where we read, 'They did not understand what he said to them' (Luke 1.30).

We know that the Holy Virgin is queen of heaven and earth, but she is more mother than queen, and people must not be made to believe (as I have often heard it said) that because of her prerogative she eclipses the glory of all the saints, just as the sun makes the stars disappear when it rises. How strange that would be! A mother who makes the glory of her children disappear! On the contrary, I believe that she increases by far the splendour of the elect.

St Thérèse of Lisieux (1873–97), *Novissima Verba*

Mary, the eschatological icon of the Church

Mary has appeared to us as the masterpiece of creation and humanity, renewed in Jesus Christ. She is the finest achievement of redemption. She never yielded to the least deviation from the divine work, and in her the saving plan of God was realized without shadow or break.

For us, Mary is the concrete proof that the grace of God is more powerful than the sin of the world.

Here on earth, in our earthly condition and even in the Church, there is always a mixture of good and evil. In contemplating Mary we have the certainty that divine grace will always gain the definitive and total victory over evil. In Mary the divine work of holiness has already been fully achieved.

In Mary the ideal of perfection to which we aspire has been realized.

Mary, refuge of sinners

That is why human beings, even great sinners, spontaneously turn to Mary, 'refuge of sinners'.

Ironic comments have often been made about the popular devotion of the faithful who seem drawn more by Mary the 'good mother' than by Christ her divine son. Certainly a marian cult, wrongly understood and detached for Christian worship, can lead to exaggerations and deviations. But does not the mass fervour in marian pilgrimages most often express the true sense of the faith of the faithful?

We implore Mary because while being, like us, a human creature of the people of the redeemed, she is the Immaculate, the wholly pure, the one who is fully conformed to the ideal of beauty and holiness to which we aspire through our innate love of the good and the beautiful.

The Declaration of Christ. Detail. Fra Angelico. Museum of S. Marco, Venice.

Ideal of a perfect humanity

Thanks to Mary, this ideal of a perfect humanity is not a distant one. It has already been realized.

Certainly it is already there, and even more, in the person of Christ, perfectly God and perfectly man. But it is as a human model that for us Mary is the goal which motivates and supports our effects towards the good: 'In Christ we find human nature led to a pre-eminent perfection in a divine person. In Mary we find the perfection which must be the very object of our desires and our efforts: the perfection of a human person like ours, taken to the highest point that a human being can attain' (Louis Bouyer, 'L'humanisme marial', *Etudes*, May 1954).

The Preface for the Mass of the Immaculate Conception puts it well: 'You chose her from all women to be our advocate with you and our pattern of holiness.'

'The eschatological figure of the church'

Mary, by her spotless holiness, anticipates and prefigures for us what the church will be when it is entirely freed from all sin at the end of the history of salvation. As the same preface says: 'Full of grace, she was to be a worthy mother of your Son, your sign of favour to the Church at its beginning, and the promise of its perfection as the bride of Christ, radiant in beauty.'

Vatican II emphasized: 'While in the most Blessed Virgin the Church has already reached that perfection whereby she exists without spot or wrinkle, the faithful still strive to conquer sin and increase in holiness. And so they turn their eyes to Mary who shines forth to the whole community of the elect as the model of virtues' (*Lumen Gentium*, 65).

A figure of the heavenly Church, Mary is the eschatological ideal towards which the Church militant must aim on its earthly pilgrimage. As Louis Bouyer writes, 'Mary is the eschatological icon of the church.'

The wonder of Bernadette

To end this meditation on the holiness of Mary, let us listen to the testimony of Bernadette of Lourdes.

To someone who asked her whether the lady was beautiful, she replied, 'Oh yes, how beautiful she is!' And when they kept on questioning her, asking, 'Is she more beautiful than Madame X or Madame Y?' (said to be the most elegant in Lourdes), Bernadette said with a smile: 'Oh, those ladies don't come anywhere near her!' Then suddenly her face turned serious and she said in a tone of wonder: 'She is so beautiful that having seen her once one would like to die to see her again.'

4
Mary and the Paschal Sacrifice

Mary, mother of the Crucified

The role of Mary in connection with the sacrifice of the cross is the extension to Calvary of the mother's mission that she assumed from the incarnation on.

So the close correlation of the motherhood of Mary with the work of redemption which we noted at the moment of the incarnation returns under the same physical aspect at the moment of the crucifixion.

It is by the gift of his life offered with love that Jesus consummated his saving work and enabled us to merit the grace of forgiveness and sanctification.

Now was not this body given for us engendered from the flesh of Mary? Did not this blood of the new covenant which Christ shed in remission of the sins of many come from the blood of Mary?

The Son of God was able to become incarnate thanks to Mary, and he could redeem us only by sacrificing the body to which Mary had given birth. So the physical motherhood of Mary co-operated in our salvation right up to Calvary.

The motherly compassion of Mary at the foot of the cross

At Calvary, this motherly co-operation for our salvation remained conscious and voluntary, as at the incarnation.

Mary repeated in suffering at the foot of the cross the mother's 'yes' which she uttered in joy at the moment of the incarnation.

Personally bound up with the destiny of her son through her motherhood, Mary was to follow Jesus to Calvary, to share in his sacrifice out of a free commitment.

Prayer to Jesus Christ. Popular imagery. Chartres. Eighteenth century.

Stabat Mater

Sequence for the feast of Our Lady of Sorrows, 15 September

By the Cross her vigil keeping
Stands the Queen of sorrows weeping,
   While her Son in torment hangs;

Now she feels – O heart afflicted
By the sword of old predicted! –
   More than all a mother's pangs.

Sad and heavy stands beside him
She who once had magnified him
   One-begotten, only born;

While she sees that rich atoning,
Long the moaning, deep the groaning
   Of her mother-heart forlorn.

Who, Christ's Mother contemplating
In such bitter anguish waiting,
   Has no human tears to shed?

Who would leave Christ's Mother, sharing
All the pain her Son is bearing
   By those tears uncomforted?

Victim-priest of Jewry's nation,
There he hangs in expiation;
   Scourge and nail have had their will;

Earth and heaven his cause forsaking,
Now his noble heart is breaking,
   Now the labouring breath is still.

Mother, fount whence love flows truest,
Let me know the pain thou knewest,
   Let me weep as thou hast wept;

Love divine within me burning,
That diviner love returning
   May thy Son this heart accept.

Mother, if my prayer be granted,
Those five wounds of his implanted
   In my breast I fain would see;

Love exceeding hangs there bleeding,
My cause pleading, my love needing –
   Bid him share his cross with me.

Till life fails, I would not fail him,
Still remember, still bewail him,
   Born thy Son, and crucified;

By the cross my vigil keeping
I would spend those hours of weeping
   Queen of sorrows, at thy side.

Virgin, boast of all creation,
Heed my tears, nor consolation
   In thy bitterness repel;

At thy side his livery wearing,
His cross bearing, his death sharing,
   Of those wounds the beads I'll tell.

Wounds of Christ, in spirit bruise me,
Chalice of his blood, bemuse me,
   Cross of Christ, be thou my stay!

Lest I burn in fires unending,
Sinless Maid, my cause befriending,
   Shield me at the judgment day!

Jesus, when earth's shadows leave me,
Through thy Mother's prayers receive me
   With the palm of victory;

When my body lies forsaken
Let my ransomed soul awaken
   Safe, in Paradise, with thee.

Attributed to Jacopone da Todi (1228–1306)
Translated by R. A. Knox

60

The Virgin being supported by the holy women. Detail of the Crucifixion. Mantegna. The Louvre, Paris.

A mother's 'yes' renewed on Calvary

The oblation which the divine Word made of himself, to his Father, by coming into this world, was consummated in the bloody sacrifice of Good Friday. 'It is fulfilled!' (John 19.30), cried Jesus before he breathed his last.

The mother's 'yes' which Mary pronounced at the moment of the incarnation, in communion with the priestly 'yes' of Jesus, was also to be consummated on Calvary.

Commitment to the redemptive sacrifice

Mary, the first to be redeemed, is also the first believer who acquiesced at the foot of the cross in the sacrifice of the Redeemer. At the presentation of Jesus in the temple, Simeon had told Mary that she was to share in the grievous fate of her child: 'A sword will pierce through your own soul' (Luke 2.35, a text quoted in *Lumen Gentium*, 57).

We find the martyrdom of the Virgin, which you will remember makes the twelfth star in her diadem, both in the prophecies of Simeon and in the story of the passion of the Lord. 'Behold this child is set for the rising of many,' said the holy old man, and, addressing Mary, he added, 'And a sword will pierce through your own soul also' (Luke 2.34–35). It is your soul, blessed mother, that the sword pierced! How could it have penetrated the flesh of your son without piercing it? And after your Jesus had held the last supper, the cruel spear which, without respecting his now senseless body, opened his side, could not reach his soul; but it was yours that it pierced. His soul was no longer in his body, but yours could not be separated from it. So the sharpness of the pain pierced your soul, and we must proclaim that you are more than martyr, since in you compassion of heart was so much stronger than passion of body.

St Bernard, *Sermon for the Sunday in the Octave of the Assumption*

The Gospel of John shows us the mother of Jesus standing (*stabat*) at the foot of the cross: 'His mother was standing by the cross of Jesus' (John 19.25). So Mary became the *mater dolorosa*, 'the mother of sorrows'.

Beyond doubt she only began to understand this sorrowful aspect of her mission as mother step by step. But on the day of the passion, when she saw Jesus crucified, herself illuminated and strengthened anew by a grace of faith, she accepted the sacrifice of her son and made a free and willing oblation of her suffering and even the offering of her son for the salvation of humankind.

She accepted, with full consent, the redemptive death of her son. This was not a simple resignation, but a real communion with the saving love of Jesus. Mary, her heart broken but full of love, succeeded at the foot of the cross in giving us her son.

Mary is in no way redemptive

The co-operation of Mary in the sacrifice of the cross has the same nature and the same intent as the co-operation she showed at the time of the incarnation. This was a role of free adherence, a 'yes' of communion with the sacrifice of the cross, the redeeming merit of which remains the face of Christ alone.

Clearly it was only the grace merited by Christ that produced in Mary, as at the annunciation, this *fiat*, this 'yes' of compassion. Christ redeemed his mother to the degree of making her capable of committing herself personally to the oblation by which, once offered, he took away the sins of the many (Heb. 9.28; 10.14).

So Mary is in no way a Redeemer along with Jesus. But she freely supported his redemptive sacrifice. It was to emphasize this close association of Mary with the work of her son that certain theologians spoke in the fourteenth century of Mary as *co-redemptrix* . Although this expression was taken up by Pius XI at one point and has been defended by some theologians of our day (a

> This union of the Mother and the Son in the work of Redemption reaches its climax on Calvary, where Christ 'offered Himself unblemished unto God' (Heb. 9.14) and where Mary stood by the Cross; there she 'shared the bitter sorrow of her only-begotten Son, associated herself to His sacrifice with the heart of a mother, and lovingly consented to the immolation of the victim which had been born of her' (*Lumen Gentium*, 58) and which she also was offering to the eternal Father. To perpetuate through the centuries the sacrifice of the Cross, the divine Saviour instituted the Eucharistic Sacrifice, the memorial of His death and Resurrection, and entrusted it to His spouse the Church, which calls the faithful together, especially upon Sundays, to celebrate the Passover of the Lord until he comes again. This the Church does in union and with the saints in heaven and in particular with the Blessed Virgin, whose burning charity and unshakable faith she imitates.
>
> *Marialis Cultus*, 20

> Thus we find ourselves at the very centre of the fulfilment of the promise contained in the Protogospel: the 'seed of the woman . . . will crush the head of the serpent' (cf. Gen. 3.15). By his redemptive death Jesus Christ conquers the evil of sin and death at its very roots. It is significant that, as he speaks to his mother from the Cross, he calls her 'woman' and says to her: 'Woman, behold your son!'. Moreover, he had addressed her by the same term at Cana too (cf. John 2.4). How can one doubt that especially now, on Golgotha, this expression goes to the very heart of the mystery of Mary, and indicates the unique place which she occupies in the whole economy of salvation? . . .
>
> . . . In this way, she who as the one 'full of grace' was brought into the mystery of Christ in order to be his Mother and thus the Holy Mother of God, through the Church remains in that mystery as 'the woman' spoken of by the Book of Genesis (3.15) at the beginning and by the Apocalypse (12.1) at the end of the history of salvation.
>
> *Redemptoris Mater*, 24

movement between the 1930s and the 1960s), it has clearly been dismissed by Vatican II.

Granted, in a broad sense *co-redemptrix* sought to signify the specific acquiescence of Mary in the redemptive sacrifice. In this broader sense one can also speak of the co-operation of all Christians in the grace of redemption by their free consent. However, the expression 'co-redemption' is unfortunate and ambiguous, since there is a risk that it will suggest that Mary plays as central a role as Christ. So Vatican II removed it.

The teaching of Vatican II

The Second Vatican Council did not want to go into these discussions, which were often very subtle. It even avoided the term 'co-redemption' which is generally misunderstood, above all by Protestants.

However, the Council retained the affirmation defended by many theologians that at the cross Mary freely involved herself in the sacrifice of Christ, the one Redeemer, by her faith, just as at the annunciation she freely involved herself in the incarnation by accepting her motherhood.

Vatican II writes: 'This union of the mother with the Son in the work of salvation is made manifest from the time of Christ's virginal conception up to his death' (*Lumen Gentium*, 57). Later on the Council makes this more specific: 'Thus the Blessed Virgin advanced in her pilgrimage of faith, and faithfully persevered in her union with her Son unto the cross, where she stood, in keeping with the divine plan, enduring with her only begotten Son the intensity of his suffering, associated herself with his sacrifice in her mother's heart, and lovingly consenting to the immolation of this victim which was born of her' (*Lumen Gentium*, 58).

Again, the Council says: 'She shared her Son's sufferings as he died on the cross. Thus, in a wholly singular way she co-operated by her

63

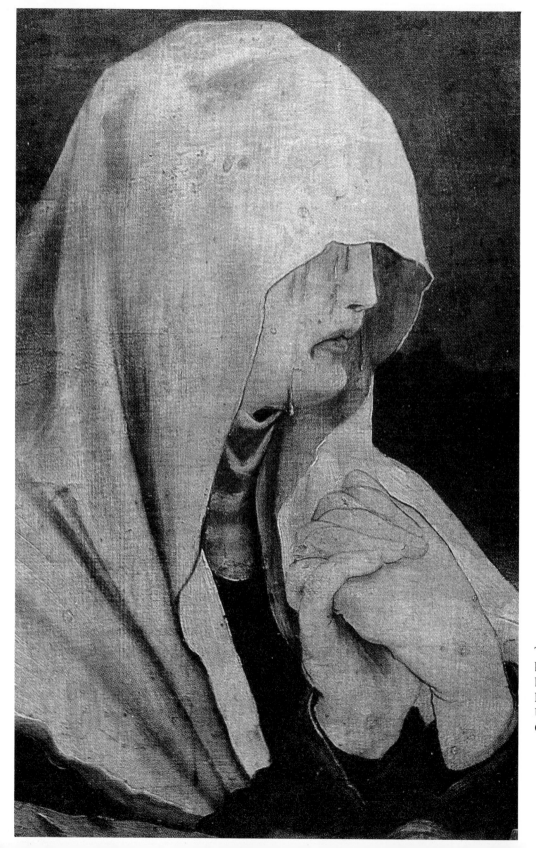

The Virgin.
Detail from the
Laying in the Tomb.
Matthias Grünewald.
Unterlinden Museum,
Colmar.

obedience, faith, hope and burning charity in the work of the Saviour in restoring supernatural life to souls. For this reason she is a mother to us in the order of grace' (*Lumen Gentium*, 58, see also *Marialis Cultus*, 20).

Mary, the 'New Eve'

By the obedience of her faith at the foot of the cross, as at the annunciation, Mary was the 'new Eve' of whom Justin and Irenaeus spoke.

Furthermore, we can think with John Paul II that the term 'woman' used by Jesus to address his mother from the cross evokes 'the woman' denoted by the book of Genesis (3.15, *Redemptoris Mater*, 24).

The ecclesial dimension of Mary's motherly compassion

If we are to understand the whole scope of this 'yes' given by Mary at the foot of the cross, we must consider it here in its ecclesial dimension.

Mary, at the foot of the cross, involved herself in the redemptive sacrifice in the name of all ransomed humanity; she is the figure of the Church there. She represents the Church, which, in its first member, can already associate itself with the sacrifice of Christ the head.

The similarity between Mary's commitment and that of the Church

We should not forget that if Jesus is the sole Redeemer, in order to benefit from this salvation gained for all, we must commit ourselves freely to this redemptive sacrifice by an active faith.

Our personal involvement in the paschal mystery of Christ is necessary if we are to pass through him and in him from death to life. St Augustine said: 'God who created you without yourself cannot save you without yourself.'

Mary's consent to the sacrifice of the cross on Golgotha was of the same nature as that of the whole Church which, in each of its members, must commit itself to the sole sacrifice of Christ made sacramentally present in the eucharistic sacrifice.

The difference between the commitment of Mary and that of the Church

However, there is a difference between the commitment of Mary to the sacrifice of Christ on Calvary and the present commitment of the whole Church.

Mary is the only member of the Church who committed herself to the sacrifice of Jesus at the very moment when it was being made on the cross, and she associated herself with it by reason of her motherhood.

Today we only give our acquiescence to the redemptive act after its tragic fulfilment. But Mary, who because she was mother of the Saviour, had a personal and immediate relationship with him, could give ecclesial assent in the very presence of Christ, who, in dying, offered his life for the salvation of humankind.

The commitment of Mary in the name of the whole Church

That is why, at the foot of the cross, Mary, as the first member of the Church, already represented the whole Church of the redeemed. By her faith she committed herself to the sacrifice of Christ the head, in the name and place of the whole Church.

Just as, at the annunciation, we welcomed Christ in Mary and through Mary, so, on Calvary, we committed ourselves to the sacrifice of Christ, in her and through her. So when today we unite ourselves with the sacrifice of Jesus, we personally renew this 'yes' that Mary pronounced first, at the foot of the cross, in all our names.

A role of consent

However, it has to be repeated that this co-operation of Mary's in the sacrifice of Calvary, like our own co-operation in redeeming grace, remained a role of active consent and commitment. Despite its direct relationship with the redemptive act, this co-operation of Mary's was not set alongside it to become a second saving act specific to Mary, so inferior and subordinate was it to that of Christ. The redemptive work of Christ is specific to him and remains undivided.

The expression 'participating in the passion of Christ', in his sacrifice, does not in any way signify that our own oblation is part of the redemptive act. It signifies that to benefit from it we should consent actively in the paschal sacrifice by agreeing to follow Jesus on the way of the cross in order with him to attain his kingdom of glory.

The faith of the Christian is not a purely passive acceptance of the fruits of redemption without involvement in the paschal mystery. The 'yes' of Christians to their salvation must be expressed through various acts of faith, of penitence, prayer and love. Their faith must be active

and spur them to imitate Christ to the point of sharing in his most intimate feelings of offering and service, as we are recommended to do by the apostle Paul in his letter to the Philippians.

This same Paul, who so strongly emphasized the uniqueness of the saving act, does not hesitate to say: 'Now I rejoice in my sufferings for your sake, and in my flesh I complete what is lacking in Christ's afflictions for the sake of his body, that is, the church' (Col. 1.24).

Once again, Mary is not the Redeemer. The co-operation of her faith, of her consent to the redeeming sacrifice, is not a co-redemption. She is not on the same level as the saving action of the one saviour, but at the level of redeemed humanity and the acts of free commitment by which human beings can and should share in the sacrifice of Christ.

So we affirm with scripture that Jesus is the sole Redeemer. Our Catholic doctrine of the association of Mary in the sacrifice of the cross, like that of the association of the whole Church, does not go beyond St Paul's assertions about justifying faith.

Justifying faith

According to St Paul, the faith which saves is not an attitude of purely passive confidence but an active commitment of the members of the ecclesial body in the paschal mystery of its head.

Many Protestants today are rediscovering this traditional doctrine of redemption and can understand the significance of a co-operation of Mary and the Church, meditating on St Paul's remarks about justifying faith.

The mystery of Mary's co-operation on the cross is also that of the whole Church, which, at the moment when it was drawn from the side of the new covenant, dying on the cross, was to unite itself with him in what St Augustine was so fond of calling 'the nuptials of the new covenant'.

66

Mater dolorosa. Icon on glass. Romania. Early nineteenth century.

Mary, representative of the ecclesial body

Beyond question Christ, as the unique mediator of humanity with the Father, represented all humanity on the cross to offer on its behalf the sacrifice which was to redeem it.

Consequently, it is Christ who brings together all the oblations of the past and the future to offer them in one perfect sacrifice of praise and reparation.

In dying on the cross Christ offered all humanity, with which he had solidarity from his incarnation in this world. The sacrifice of Jesus is the perfect sacrifice of humanity.

However, we must also say that the divine Word was not willing to incorporate himself in humanity without its free consent. Similarly on Calvary, although he was the one and perfect representative of humanity before the Father and had no need of any help or any instrument to offer his sacrifice, Christ the head wanted the free commitment of the whole of his ecclesial body: Mary, at the foot of the cross, gave that commitment.

During the mass, the faithful must unite themselves by their personal oblation with the sacrifice which the priest offers sacramentally, as representative of Christ the Head. Similarly, Mary, by her motherly compassion, acquiesced for all humanity in the sacrifice of which Christ, the one representative of humanity before the Father, was the unique priest. Jesus represented humanity as head, by offering himself for the salvation of humankind. Mary represented humanity as the first member of the mystical body of the Church: she had to offer consent to the sacrifice of Christ in the name of all the others.

The oblation of Mary, the oblation of the members, was in no way redemptive. However, it was desired by Christ the head as a sign of communion with his redemptive offering.

Only Christ could, by offering himself as a sacrifice, make his ecclesial body capable of offering itself in the person of Mary.

Mary is not a priest in the ministerial sense

Mary at the foot of the cross was not a priest in the sense that a priest at the mass is a minister of the eucharistic sacrifice. Even if the expression *virgo sacerdos*, virgin priest, has been employed by venerable spiritual authors with the necessary nuances and restrictions, it is prone to wrong interpretation which can lead to senseless deviations. Has not in fact devotion to the virgin priest led to representations of the Virgin Mary clothed in priestly vestments at the foot of the cross?

On 15 January 1913 the Holy Office prohibited the publication of such pictures. Then devotion to the Virgin as priest was censured in a letter of 10 March 1927 addressed by Cardinal Merry de Val to the Bishop of Adria. Devotion to the Virgin as priest could have suggested that Mary received priestly ordination and that she was a minister of the sacrifice of Christ like the priest at the mass. However, at the moment of his sacrifice Christ had no need of any minister to represent him in sacrificial manner as at the mass. Furthermore the attribution of a ministerial priesthood to Mary would add nothing to the excellence of her prerogatives. As mother of Christ the priest, the mother of all priests, does not Mary surpass all ordained priests in dignity?

Mary and the priesthood of the baptized

However, it can quite rightly be said that by her oblation at the foot of the cross Mary, without being a priest in the sense in which we understand the presbyteral ministry, was the perfect type and ideal representative of the universal priesthood of all baptized Christians. These, without being ministers of the eucharistic sacrifice, are called to participate in it personally as members of a Church which in its entirety must associate itself with the sacrifice of Christ its head.

At each mass it is always in communion with Mary that the faithful associate themselves with the sacrifice of Christ; so it has quite rightly been said that at each celebration of the eucharistic sacrifice Mary does not cease to unite herself with the whole church in the one redeeming sacrifice of the cross.

Mary, type of the church

So Mary is certainly the type of the church. Here again we note how the privileges of Mary are only the realization *meliori modo*, 'in a better way', immediate and intensive, of prerogatives which the church receives only successively and progressively in the course of the centuries and which it will only possess totally and perfectly at the end of time.

Mary's Immaculate Conception allows in her the application, in a preventative and preservative way, of a salvation gained for all, but from which others benefit only at baptism after being born with original sin.

Her assumption will be a prefiguration of the resurrection of the whole Church when it arrives at its glorious end. Similarly, the association of Mary with the redemptive sacrifice brought about the association of the whole Church, already accomplished in Mary in the best and most immediate way at the very moment when Christ was dying on the cross.

Mary's commitment to the paschal mystery

At the end of these reflections on the compassion of Mary on Calvary, we must emphasize the paschal significance of the sacrifice of the cross to which Mary consented by a commitment that was both personal and ecclesial. Mary, at the foot of the cross, committed herself to the paschal mystery of salvation.

The death and resurrection of Christ are not to be separated

The event of the death of Christ celebrated on Good Friday must never be dissociated from the event of his glorious resurrection celebrated at Easter.

These two events, commemorated successively in liturgical time, together constitute a unique mystery of salvation, the paschal mystery of Christ, who, by his death, passed into the glory of the Father (John 13.1).

The resurrection is not a simple appendix to the life of Jesus nor a simple epilogue to the drama of redemption. The resurrection of Christ, like his death, is an integral part of the mystery of redemption. This incorporation is particularly manifest in the Gospel of John, in which the elevation of Jesus on the cross is bound up with his elevation and glorification at the right hand of the Father. The crucifixion and glorious resurrection are for John one and the same indivisible event (John 3.14; 12.32–34).

This link between the passion and the glorification is so close that Jesus could say when Judas went out of the upper room to betray him: 'Now is the Son of Man glorified and God is glorified through him' (John 13.31).

So not all the weight of redemption should be put on the cross. Certainly the resurrection of Christ does not have any meritorious character. It does not add anything to the inestimable work of the earthly life of Christ and his death on the cross. It was by the oblation of the whole of his earthly life fulfilled in the sacrifice of the cross that Jesus merited both his glorious resurrection and our justification. However, even as a meritorious work, the redemptive death of Christ is inseparable from his resurrection. It is in earning

69

Calvary. Van der Weyden. El Escorial.

for himself his glorious resurrection that Jesus earned for us saving justification. It is in being worthy to be raised as the head of a humanity justified by him and taken up with him in his passage to the kingdom of the Father that Jesus has earned our salvation.

The resurrection of Jesus signifies that his sacrifice is definitely acceptable to the Father (Heb. 9.12). The resurrection is the approval by the Father of the witness of Jesus and his redemptive work. In raising Jesus God has done him justice. The one who had been rejected and executed by the leaders of his people has been manifested by his resurrection as the Holy and Just One (Acts 3.14–15).

In this way God confirms the message of Jesus, that of the coming of the kingdom of God. The crucifixion of Jesus was not an absurd end, followed by the resurrection, but appeared as the beginning of a new world.

The glorified Christ makes us benefit from the redemptive fruits of his life and passion. The risen Christ, in sending us the Holy Spirit, gives us divine and redemptive grace (John 7.37–39; 7.1–2).

Christ was already in principle, from the incarnation, our perfect mediator with the Father. But it was when he had risen that he entered into the full exercise of his mediating and sanctifying function (Rom. 1.3–4).

It is the risen Christ who has become the 'firstborn from among the dead' (Col. 1.18), the Lord who draws all men to him (John 12.32). It is the risen Christ who makes humankind the fullness of his body, the Church (Eph. 1.20–23).

St Paul, the theologian of the redeeming death of Christ, never detaches this from the resurrection. For him, to have faith is to believe in God who 'raised from the dead Jesus our Lord, who was put to death for our trespasses and rose for our justification' (Rom. 4.24).

The link between the death and resurrection of Christ is powerfully attested in the Easter preface: 'By dying he destroyed our death; by rising he restored our life.'

This link between the sacrifice of the cross and the resurrection is brought out throughout the liturgy of Good Friday and Easter. The death of Christ is already celebrated on Good Friday as a victorious death, and the resurrection is celebrated on Easter Day as the exaltation of Jesus, who, in order to attain glory, had to pass through sacrificial death and be glorified in the wounds of his passion.

Every time that we celebrate the eucharistic sacrifice, that paschal mystery of death and resurrection is made present sacramentally.

The glorified Christ does not die again. It is the risen Christ who is present in the eucharist. But the risen Christ makes himself present when we make memorial of his death, under the signs of the bread which represents his body given for us and the wine which represents his blood, shed for many for the remission of sins.

The eucharistic sacrifice makes us share in the paschal mystery of Christ. It makes us participate in the death of Christ who has passed to his glorious risen life.

We participate in the death of Christ who makes us die to sin. We already participate in the resurrection of Christ who animates us with the divine life of his Spirit, the present pledge of our future bodily resurrection in his own glory (Rom. 6.2–4, 8–11).

Mary's commitment to the paschal sacrifice

If with the resurrection the sacrifice of the cross constitutes a single mystery of salvation, the paschal mystery, Mary, at least by an implicit faith, committed herself to the redemptive sacrifice as a paschal sacrifice.

Mary, on Calvary, could not explicitly know the paschal significance of the death of Jesus. Beyond question she was unaware that by his resurrection her son was to win an immediate victory over death.

Like the Jews of her time, the Sadducees excepted, she believed in a glorious resurrection which would arrive for the righteous at the end of

Mater dolorosa. Icon on glass. Romania. Early nineteenth century.

time. But did she know that her son was already going to be raised in anticipation of this final resurrection?

However, in spite of the apparent failure of the crucifixion, Mary, at the foot of the cross, did not lose trust. In the obedience of her faith she preserved the hope that God would do justice to her son, who had been rejected by men. Despite the cruel disappointment to the words which had been spoken to her at the annunciation, she maintained the hope that the messianic promises of salvation would be realized.

In fact the resurrection of Jesus was the fulfilment of the promises of the Old Testament. In the risen Jesus, God fulfilled the hopes of Israel in a definitive victory of life over death (Ps. 16.10–11; 73.23–24; Dan. 12.1–2; II Macc. 7.9).

By committing herself to the mystery of the crucifixion, Mary thus at least implicitly committed herself to the mystery of the resurrection. Her commitment to the cross was a commitment to the paschal mystery of salvation, even if only the light of Easter was to allow her to recognize clearly the significance of the death of her son.

Mary herself experienced this paschal significance when, at her death, by her blessed assumption she could participate in the glorious resurrection of Jesus.

In the next chapter we shall in fact see that Mary, by her commitment as mother, was associated with the paschal sacrifice of her son and was also, according to the divine plan, to be associated at her death with the risen Christ in her glorious assumption.

5

The Assumption of Mary

The significance of the dogma of the Assumption

On 1 November 1950, the feast of All Saints, in the presence of a vast crowd, estimated at a million, and surrounded by seven hundred bishops, Pius XII defined the assumption of Mary as a divinely revealed dogma.

This belief was not new, and many Catholics were astonished, since for centuries the Assumption had been celebrated on 15 August. This truth belonged to a tradition common to both East and West. It was part of the universal faith of the Church.

In 1943, Pius XII had already echoed this tradition in the marian epilogue to his encyclical on the mystical body: Mary 'reigns in heaven with her Son, her body and soul refulgent with heavenly glory'.

The mystery of the queenship of Mary is one with the glorious Assumption, even if Mary as Queen of Heaven is the object of a special festival instituted by Pius XII in 1954 (encyclical *Ad Caeli Reginam* of 11 October 1954).

The text of the definition of the Assumption, quoted in the box on this page, is taken up by Vatican II, which also mentions the title 'queen'.

'The Immaculate Virgin, preserved free from all stain of original sin, was taken up body and

> After much prayer offered in supplication to God, much invocation of the Holy Spirit, to the glory of God omnipotent, who has bestowed on the Blessed Virgin so great a favour, to the honour of his Son, the King of ages, the immortal, conqueror of sin and death, to the greater praise of this same holy Mother, and to the joy and jubilee of the whole Church, by the authority of our Lord Jesus Christ, and of his blessed Apostles Peter and Paul, and by the authority granted to us, we proclaim it, we declare it, we define it, as a doctrine divinely revealed: That the immaculate ever-virgin Mother of God, her earthly life ended, was taken up, body and soul of her, into the glory of heaven.
>
> *Munificentissimus Deus*

soul into heavenly glory, when her earthly life was over and exalted by the Lord as Queen over all things, that she might be the more fully conformed to her Son, the Lord of Lords (cf. Rev. 19.16) and conqueror of sin and death' (*Lumen Gentium*, 59).

Mary was received body and soul into heavenly glory. This sober affirmation does not go into theological explanations about the glorious condition of the human person and the nature of her transfigured body.

Avoiding spatial language

The dogmatic definition avoids all spatial language. The kingdom of God is not situated above, in heaven, in the physical sense, in some planet or star of the firmament. The glorified Virgin and her risen Son do not dwell in one or other of the galaxies.

We speak of heavenly life in order to express the superiority of a glorious eternal life to our terrestrial and temporal life.

We must be on our guard against the legendary representations given by the apocryphal gospels. At the end of the fifth century these described how Mary was carried up to heaven by angels. The apostles had come, Thomas even from India, transported by clouds, so that they could all be present at this apotheosis of Mary. Even today artists represent the scene of the assumption of Mary in this way on icons or mosaics. These illustrations of sacred art are legitimate and even necessary to evoke this mystery of Mary, but we must take them for what they are: symbolic imagery.

However, it must be emphasized that the glorified body is not situated in a heaven that can be located, and the glorious resurrection of the body is not the reanimation of a corpse, like the resurrection of Lazarus. It is a supernatural transfiguration of the human body which cannot be the object of natural experience or of any scientific explanation.

Mary's privilege

This glorious assumption of Mary, realized at the end of her earthly life, was a privilege for her in the sense in which we have already considered her Immaculate Conception as the first privilege that God conferred on her. The glorification of the body which will be ours at the end of time was anticipated for Mary at the end of her earthly life.

The saints, purified from all the consequences of sin, can obtain the glory of the beatific vision of God without waiting for the end of time. Pope Benedict XII defined this in the constitution *Benedictus Deus* of 1336.

But the resurrection of the body in its glorious transfiguration according to the traditional faith attested by the scriptures will only come about for all humankind at the end of this world.

We leave aside the question of the possibility of an immediate resurrection of the human body, a possibility which at present is being discussed by theologians. This would be the beginning of the resurrection of the body brought about for each person after death, a new relationship of our spiritual person with the created world. Whatever is made of this hypothesis, the glorious resurrection of our body, which implies, like that of Christ, a royal domination over all the cosmos and a capacity for personal and direct communication with all members of humanity, will take place only at the moment of what is called the 'general' resurrection, at the *parousia* of the Lord.

For Mary, this glorification of the body takes effect from the end of her earthly life. Certainly Pius XII did not define Mary as the sole member of the Church who has already been physically glorified. But the preambles to his definition do bear witness, in conformity to the tradition of the Church, that the assumption of Mary is a privilege. This was accorded her in anticipation of the collective and future destiny of humanity, by reason of her divine motherhood.

So it would be over-hasty to affirm, as has been done recently, that the glorious assumption of Mary is not only the figure of what the Church will be at the end of history, but also already represents the glorious condition in which all the saints of heaven now are.

On this feast of All Saints 1950, Pius XII certainly did not have the intention of defining the glorious assumption of all the saints. The precise object of his dogmatic definition was solely the anticipatory glorification of Mary.

Assumption
of the Virgin.
Saint Riquier.
Fifteenth century.

Mary's death

However, in his definition Pius XII did not touch on the question of the death of Mary, which is still discussed by theologians. Still, if we look at the doctrinal preambles of the definition, it seems that the general opinion is that Mary died before being transfigured in glory.

The glorification of her body would then be its resurrection, even if the text of the definition does not speak of the 'risen Mary'.

According to the liturgy itself, the ancient names for the feast of the Assumption, *Transitus virginis, Dormitio, Depositio,* certainly indicate that Mary truly died. So the assumption, like the ascension of Christ, is a resurrection of the body.

However, we can go more deeply into this question of the death of Mary today in the context of a theology of human death.

The two aspects of human death

Human death can be envisaged under two aspects. As biological death, it is the natural death of the whole earthly body. In its earthly condition the human body is by nature mortal, like any animal body. One cannot say that this biological death is the consequence of sin for human beings. It is the obligatory passage from earthly life to heavenly life.

On the other hand, by reason of sin, for human beings death has the aspect of being a more or less dramatic crucifying break. For the biblical writers, biological death can take on the significance of an eternal death, i.e. an eternal break with God, in the state of damnation. For contemporary atheism, biological death has even become the sign of a total and eternal destruction of the human person, which is returned to nothingness. It is this tragic interpretation of human death that is the consequence of our sin.

The death of Christ

Jesus did not only experience biological human death as the obligatory passage to the immortal and glorious life of the kingdom of God.

By becoming involved through his incarnation in a sinful world, Jesus freely accepted the confrontation with sin and death on the cross as its victim. By consenting to die the victim of human sin, he willed to offer his life for our salvation. So his death was a sacrificial death. By his death Jesus not only won the victory of divine eternal life over biological human death; by his redemptive oblation he also won the victory of love over hatred and sin. His oblation of infinite love was able to triumph over all the refusals of love in the form of sins committed by humanity in the course of its earthly history.

The death of Mary, a joyous assumption

To return to the death of Mary: like Christ and every other human being, Mary had to experience death as the passage to the life of glory. But did not the one who is mother of Christ the Redeemer also have to participate in the death of Christ as a sacrificial and redemptive death? Did not Jesus say that to attain to glory, every human being must follow his example and endure the cross? This requirement indubitably applied to Mary, as to Christ the Redeemer and all the redeemed who have to participate in the paschal mystery of Jesus before attaining to glory.

However, was not Mary closely associated with the redemptive sacrifice when, standing at the foot of the cross, with the most extraordinary maternal compassion she became the mother of sorrows?

As a consequence of what I said earlier about the role of Mary on Calvary, and with many theologians, I think that since Mary was associated at the foot of the cross with the sacrificial death of Christ, at the moment of her biological death she did not have to experience the sacrificial aspect of human death.

The Sleep
of the Virgin.
Benozzo
Gozzoli.
Vatican.

So Mary truly died at the end of her earthly life. But beyond doubt her death was a joyful and exultant passage to the glorious life. Her indubitable death was, I think, a joyous assumption, experienced in a kind of beatific ecstasy, without any painful break, for Mary had already experienced the cross, at the foot of the cross of Jesus.

The foundation of the definition of the Assumption: the universal faith of the Church

No explicit scriptural attestation or oral tradition

Holy Scripture says nothing about the assumption of Mary. Whereas the resurrection of Jesus is attested to us by the accounts of his appearances, the assumption of Mary is not mentioned by any explicit scriptural testimony.

Furthermore, unlike the resurrection of Jesus, the assumption of Mary is not the foundation of our hope in the resurrection but only a fruit of the resurrection, of Jesus who contributes to strengthening our hope.

The constitution *Munificentissimus Deus* of Pius XII does not resort to any biblical text as a basis for an explicit attestation of the assumption of Mary. Nor does it appeal to an oral tradition.

The universal faith of the Church

To define the dogma of the Assumption, the pope based himself on the universal faith of the Church, which is indefectible, and on its universal teaching.

This living faith of the Church is particularly evident in the liturgy, but it is also attested by the doctors and the theologians.

So the pope began from the expression of the universal faith of the Church manifested over the ages from the sixth century.

The definition therefore stems from a development lasting for centuries and was the object of a long preparation.

The preparation of the definition

Numerous petitions for the definition, coming above all from English Catholics, were addressed to Pius XII. He entrusted a study of the question to expert theologians already known for their wise work on the assumption, like Fr Balic, the Franciscan, and Fr Jugie, an assumptionist Augustinian. But all theologians were invited to communicate their views.

Then, on 1 May 1946, Pius XII addressed a letter, *Deiparae Virginis Mariae*, to the bishops of the whole world in communion with the Holy See.

He put this question to them: 'In your wisdom and prudence, do you think that the bodily assumption of the blessed Virgin could be proposed and defined as a dogma of faith, and do you, your clergy and your faithful want this?' 98.2% of the replies were affirmative. Only twenty-two replies were negative, sixteen of which only challenged the timing of the definition and six of which expressed doubts on the possibility of a definition.

We should note that according to the statistics for the seventeen oriental churches linked to the

Holy See, fifty-four responses of Eastern patriarchs and residential bishops were affirmative and just one negative.

So the definition of the dogma of the Assumption is based on the faith of the church expressed in its universal tradition.

The authority of tradition in the Church

The essential question here is that of the authority of tradition in the Church. It is this that still divides Protestants and Catholics today. Christ did not entrust his gospel to a book which he wrote, but charged his Church to hand it down, promising the Church the presence of the Holy Spirit.

In its dogmatic constitution *Dei Verbum* Vatican II stipulated what is the transmission by the Church of the divine revelation and what are the mutual relations between scripture and the Church's tradition.

So here there is a basic certainty: the universal Church is preserved from all error in what it teaches or what it believes in, in such a way that on the one hand the universal *magisterium* can only teach and on the other all the faithful can only believe as a truth revealed by God what is contained in the deposit of revelation.

When the Church teaches and believes universally that a truth is revealed, this truth is in fact revealed and belongs at least implicitly, in nucleus, to the deposit of revelation.

Now the heavenly glorification of the body of Mary is a supernatural fact which cannot be known by the natural light of our faculty or by historical experience. It can only be known by divine revelation, and since the Church in fact believes it, this is revealed.

Otherwise one would have to question the presence of the Holy Spirit which was promised by Jesus to his Church, to transmit the divine revelation in an authentic way.

The witnesses of the Church's tradition

If it is the universal faith of the Church, that of the teaching *magisterium* and of all the faithful believers, which guarantees that the assumption of Mary belongs to the tradition of revelation, it is important to take stock of the main witness to this Church tradition.

Pius XII's constitution is for the most part devoted to precisely this.

Testimonies of the Christian life

Pius XII first of all evokes the testimonies of the life of the Christian people: numerous churches are dedicated to the assumption and many pictorial works represent it.

> It was necessary that she who had preserved her virginity without stain in childbirth should preserve her body without corruption even after death. It was necessary that she who had borne the Creator as a child in her womb should dwell in the divine tabernacles. It was necessary that the bride to whom the Father was united should dwell in heaven. It was necessary that she who had seen her Son on the Cross and had escaped the sword of pain in bringing him into the world, who had received him in her womb, should see him still sitting with his Father. It was necessary that the Mother of God should possess all that appertains to her Son and that she should be honoured by all creatures as the Mother of God and his servant.
> St John of Damascus, Homely II on *Dormitionem BV Mariae*

Pius XII writes: 'Cities, dioceses and countries have entrusted their safety to the patronage of God's Virgin Mother raised to heaven; religious institutes have been founded, with the Church's sanction, taking their name from that special title. It is significant, too, that in the devotion of the Holy Rosary . . . one of the mysteries prescribed for meditation is, as we all know, that of our Lady's Assumption into heaven' (*Munificentissimus Deus*).

'You appeared, as it is written, in splendour; and your virginal body is entirely holy, entirely chaste, entirely the dwelling-place of God; in such form that by virtue of this fact it is then exempt from falling into dust. Transformed in its humanity into a sublime life of incorruptibility, living and most glorious, intact and participating in the perfect life.

St Germain of Constantinople, Sermon I,
In Dormitionem Deiparae

The liturgical tradition

Then the liturgical tradition is invoked. The feast of the Assumption is mentioned in the Western sacramentaries from the Carolingian period on. It was celebrated in the Eastern liturgy from an even earlier date, from the sixth century.

First of all celebrated as the feast of the Dormition, its original object was the death of Mary. However, the notion of the incorruptibility of her body and her elevation to heavenly glory soon emerged. The idea of the bodily assumption is formally attested in the liturgical texts of the eighth and ninth centuries.

Under the influence of Pseudo-Jerome, there were hesitations as to whether the assumption of the body was part of the content of the festival. However, from the high Middle Ages the affirmative point of view won the day.

The testimonies of the theological doctors

Pius XII then examines the testimonies of the Fathers, doctors and theologians who specify the object of this cult and prove that it is in accord with revealed truths. 'To say that the body of the Blessed Virgin never knew decay, was not to exhaust the meaning of this solemnity. What we celebrated was the triumph she won over death when she was glorified, after the pattern of her only Son Jesus Christ, up in heaven.'

There are many of these testimonies: in the sixteenth century, St Robert Bellarmine, St Peter Canisius and St Francis of Sales; in the fifteenth century, St Bernardine of Siena; in the Middle Ages, St Bonaventure, St Thomas Aquinas and St Albert the Great, without forgetting St Amadeus, Bishop of Lausanne, at the beginning of the scholastic theology.

These testimonies go back to the eighth century with St John of Damascus and the seventh century with St Germanus of Constantinople, whose texts have remained famous. They already present the assumption of Mary in relation to her other gifts and privileges.

The apocryphal texts

Going even further back, we come to the apocryphal texts of the fifth and perhaps even the fourth centuries. These are the first documents to attest the Church's belief in the assumption of Mary. Pius XII does not speak of them and they have no official value. But it is not unworthy that a truth of faith should first have been expressed in works made up of legends.

For want of historical documents, when belief in the assumption came to be expressed, there was a concern to provide a foundation for it by inventing stories which represented the assumption of Mary.

Although these apocryphal documents have no historical authenticity, they attest that belief in the assumption was already well implanted among Christian people, who recognized it as true.

No formal testimony during the first centuries

If we go back further, to the first centuries of the Church, we find absolutely nothing on the subject.

This absence of testimony poses a problem on which we must dwell. How could this truth of the assumption of Mary, belief in which is well attested in the sixth century, have been known? The Church has made no pronouncement on the method of the transmission of the revealed truth of the assumption.

Some theologians have wanted to resolve the problem by presupposing a local oral tradition which would have gone back to the apostles and gradually spread through the Church. This is not unthinkable. But we have no trace of such a tradition in the first Christian writers. So it is a mere hypothesis.

However, in establishing the revealed character of a truth of faith it is not necessary that it should explicitly be contained in scripture, nor even that it should have been made the object of explicit belief in the very first centuries.

It is enough that it should be contained implicitly in the deposit of revelation. Moreover it is not necessary that from the beginning of the apostolic Church Christians should have become aware that the assumption of Mary was implied in the mystery of her motherhood.

Only later could the Church come to this awareness, and for that the following two conditions are enough.

No denial of the assumption in the first centuries

First, it is enough that during the first centuries there was never any formal denial of the assumption nor affirmation of the corruption of Mary's body.

There was never a cult of relics of Mary. No recollection was ever handed down of a place where her body had been preserved, and where there were claims to have found her tomb, it was empty.

St Bernadine of Siena, cited by Pius XII, uses this argument: 'How do we account for the fact that the Church has never tried to find any relics of the Blessed Virgin, or exposed such relics to veneration? This may even be described as a kind of "empirical proof".'

This argument is strong when we are aware that Christian people passionately sought out the relics of saints.

So the question of the assumption of Mary remained open.

The living awareness of the Church

For belief in the assumption to be expressed explicitly in the Church, it was enough on the other hand that at a moment in history Christians should have discovered that the truth of the assumption of Mary was implied in the truth of her virgin motherhood.

In fact St Germanus of Constantinople in the sixth century and St John of Damascus in the eighth showed that the assumption of Mary was fitting for her motherhood and the specific holiness of her virginal body.

Through their two texts, quoted in boxes, we see how what we now call the development of the dogma came about.

The development of the dogma and the analogy of faith

It is a matter of becoming aware of a revealed truth not affirmed explicitly in scripture, from other truths taught formally which contain it implicitly.

This is what is also called the analogy of faith. Plenary revelation forms a global whole, the revealed truths of which are linked together in the indivisibility of a single revealed mystery, that of the economy of salvation.

This was realized concretely according to the divine plan in the person of Christ, Son of God incarnate in Mary, who died and rose again for us.

As for Mary, one can emphasize the deep parallels between all her privileges: motherhood, virginity, association with the saving work of Christ her son, and her assumption.

These are not logical deductions that we could claim on more or less compelling grounds, as being fitting. Here is expression of an awareness of the place that Mary, as mother of the Saviour, in fact occupied in the economy of salvation. The aim is to show that all the truths believed and taught by the church on the subject of Mary are harmonious in this global revelation of salvation realized in Jesus Christ, born of Mary.

As Pius XII wrote: 'From all eternity, the Blessed Virgin has been the object of God's unique loving regard; and when at last the appointed time came, his Providence saw to it that all the gifts and graces freely bestowed on her should be characterized by a kind of inner coherence.'

The assumption of Mary, immaculate from her conception

Pius XII shows the parallel between the privilege of the Immaculate Conception and that of the assumption of Mary.

'After all, there was the closest possible bond between the two. Christ, by his own death, overcame death as well as sin, and through him the supernatural rebirth given us in baptism puts death as well as sin behind us; but it is not God's will that this triumph over death should be realized, for the redeemed in general, until the end of the world . . . From this general law God would have the Blessed Virgin exempt. Immaculately conceived, by God's unique dispensation, she rose superior to sin; on her, then, the general law was not binding – not for her the tomb's decay, not for her to wait till the Day of Judgment before her body could be redeemed.

The solemn declaration once made that God's Virgin Mother was set free, thus early, from the guilty taint of her race, what wonder if hope beat high among Christian people that the living voice of the Church would define, without further ado, the doctrine of her bodily Assumption?'

Vatican II also underlines this link between the Immaculate Conception and the assumption: 'The Immaculate Virgin, preserved from all stain of original sin, was taken up body and soul into heavenly glory' (*Lumen Gentium*, 59).

The assumption of Mary, ever virgin

Mary remained ever virgin. Since she had remained virgin until her motherhood, it was not fitting that subsequently God should have abandoned the virginal body of his mother to the corruption of the tomb.

St John of Damascus wrote: 'It was necessary

that she who had kept her virginity in childbirth should keep her body without corruption, even after death.' And Pius XII points out that St Germanus of Constantinople thought that the incorruption of the body of the Virgin Mary, mother of God, and her elevation to heaven, were not only fitting for her divine motherhood, but even also to the particular holiness of her virginal body.

As St Germanus wrote: 'Her virgin body is entirely holy, entirely chaste, entirely the dwelling place of God; in such a way that by this fact it is then exempt from falling into dust, transformed in its humanity into a sublime life of incorruptibility, itself living and most glorious, intact and participating in the perfect life.'

The assumption of Mary, the New Eve

From the second century, with St Justin and St Irenaeus, the Fathers saw Mary as the New Eve.

Just as Eve had been vanquished by the serpent, so in Mary the serpent was vanquished. Eve had been dealt a double death by the serpent, that of sin and that of bodily corruption. By her Immaculate Conception Mary was exempt from sin. By her assumption she will also be exempt from corruption. It is by virtue of this double exemption that Mary is truly the New Eve.

Pius XII notes the close union of the New Eve and the New Adam in the struggle and the victory.

'It is to be remembered that, from the second century onwards, our Lady has been indentified by the Fathers of the Church as the Second Eve. Not on the same level, indeed, as the Second Adam, but intimately associated in his warfare against the Enemy of our race. It was to issue, as we know from the Promise made in Paradise, in a complete triumph over sin and death, those twin enemies that are so often coupled together by St Paul. Of this victory, our Lord's Resurrection is the operative part, the supreme trophy; but our Lady, too, who shared in the conflict, must share in its conclusion, through the glorifying of that virgin body of hers. Only then, as the Apostle says, "when this mortal nature wears its immortality, the saying of scripture will come true, Death is swallowed up in victory" (I Cor. 15.54).'

If Mary, the New Eve, was associated at the foot of the cross with the redemptive sacrifice by which the Christ, the New Adam, gained the victory over sin and death, it was fitting that at the moment of her own death she should also be associated with the victory of Jesus over death.

However, we must never lose sight of the fact that this association of Mary with Christ, in all the phases of the economy of salvation, is always based on her motherhood. The motherhood of Mary is the fundamental justification for her assumption and all the other privileges with which that of the assumption is closely linked.

The Virgin. Russian icon. Detail.

The assumption of Mary, mother of the risen Christ

At the interface between two articles of faith

The dogma of the Assumption relates to two articles of faith: the general resurrection of human beings at the end of time and the divine motherhood of Mary.

As mother of Christ, Mary exists in an immediate personal relationship with Christ. She is associated closely and indissolubly with Christ the Head. It follows from this that she was able to participate in an immediate way in the resurrection of Christ her son, without any delay, at the moment of her death.

As I have said, the privilege of the assumption of Mary does not reside in her glorious resurrection itself. It is a prerogative that the whole Church will know at the end of time (I Cor. 15.20–26, the second reading of the mass of Pentecost). But the privilege of Mary consists in the fact that for her this resurrection is realized immediately after death.

Mary's Immaculate Conception was the realization in her, *meliori modo*, in the best way, by anticipation, of the redemption realized through baptism for all the other members of the church.

Similarly, for Mary her assumption was the realization *meliori modo*, in the best way, by anticipation, of the glorious resurrection which will be realized through baptism for all the other members of the church at the end of history.

The mother, associate of the Redeemer

From the incarnation to the paschal sacrifice of the cross, Mary did not cease, by reason of her motherhood, to be associated with the person of Christ and his saving mission. The mother of the risen Christ, she was equally to remain closely associated with him immediately after her death.

As Pius XII writes: 'In the last resort, all these Fathers, all these theologians, base their conclusions on the Bible, which has given us the picture of our Lord's Mother as inseparably attached to her Divine Son, and constantly sharing his lot. It seems impossible to imagine her as apart from him after death, in body any more than in soul, the Mother who conceived and bore and suckled him, who carried him in her arms and clasped him to her breast. Her Son, he could not but love and honour her next to his eternal Father, whose law he kept so perfectly; and since it lay in his power to pay her this supreme honour, of sparing her from the ravages of the tomb, we must needs believe that he did so.'

The preface to the mass of the Assumption of Mary celebrates her in this way: 'You would not allow decay to touch her body, for she had given birth to your Son, the Lord of all life.'

However, we can understand that it took a certain period of reflection for the Church in its faith really to become aware that the assumption of Mary was implied in the mystery of her motherhood.

It is remarkable that belief in the assumption of Mary was expressed clearly only after the recognition of the dogma of the divine motherhood. To recognize the glorious assumption of Mary, was it not necessary first of all to believe that Mary was truly mother of God, *theotokos*?

The assumption of Mary, mother of all human beings

If the dogma of the Assumption of Mary is first of all associated with that of his divine motherhood, it would also seem to be closely associated with the traditional doctrine of Mary's spiritual motherhood of all human beings.

Would Mary today be totally our mother if for us she was only a saint glorified in her body but still waiting for bodily glorification? Could Mary personally and directly know each one of us as her child if she had not already attained the glory of the resurrection?

The glorious resurrection of human beings at the end of time will include participation in the reign of the risen Christ over the whole of creation and will also offer the possibility of direct and personal communication with all existing members of the human community.

It does not seem that those who are dead, even the greatest saints, are already capable of such a royal and universal relationship.

The assumption of Mary, the condition of her universal intercession

The Virgin Mary is already capable of entering into a personal, immediate and direct communion with each one of us, and she knows us by name. Unlike the intercession of the other saints, her motherly mediation is universal, as I shall be pointing out in the next chapter (p. 105), precisely by reason of the fact that she already participates in the ascension and the glorious kingdom of the risen Christ.

If by this universal awareness Mary can know each of us as her own child, it is because, having attained the glory of the resurrection, she has been made capable of such a personal relation-ship with all the members of the Church. At the moment of her elevation in soul and body to the heavenly glory, Mary, already our mother from the incarnation on, had become fully aware of this spiritual motherhood.

From her glorious assumption, then, Mary, has been able to exercise her motherly interces-sion in a universal way, on behalf of each member of humanity.

As Pius XII said, 'the main principle on which the royal dignity of Mary rests is without doubt her Divine Motherhood' (Encyclical on the Queenship of Mary, *Ad Caeli Reginam*, 1954).

The definition of the Assumption – an opportunity or an obstacle to unity?

So the assumption of Mary was a truth which belonged to the deposit of revelation. But a second question arises: was it opportune to define it as a dogma of faith?

Some Catholics thought that while it was possible to define the assumption, the promulgation of this dogma was not desirable at the time. They were considering the reactions it would provoke in some Protestant churches.

Protestant reactions

The definition did in fact provoke a feeling among Protestants in some countries which was near to outrage, and Pastor Boegner, one of the presidents of the World Council of Churches, several times pronounced grave words on the matter.

Pius XII had foreseen this reaction, but despite his paternal concern for all the churches, he did not let it stop him. First of all, it must be said that it was for the pope to be the judge of this opportunity.

The Church has a mission of truth

Then one can recall that the Church's mission is a mission of truth which it has to proclaim 'in season and out of season' (II Tim. 4.2). If the assumption of Mary was an article of the faith of the Church, a truth bound up with its belief in the general resurrection and in the motherhood of Mary, mother of Christ and mother of all human beings, did not the Church have to proclaim it without necessarily taking account of all possible reactions?

Invitation to a true ecumenical dialogue

In fact, if first of all this definition seemed to put an obstacle in the way of efforts towards ecumenism, was it not an invitation to a more authentic dialogue between Catholics and Protestants, by putting at the heart of the debate what still divides them: the question of the living tradition of the Church and its relation to scripture?

This fundamental problem was to be taken up and illuminated by Vatican II in its constitution *Dei Verbum* which, from the ecumenical point of view, was hailed as the most important document of the council.

It would be necessary above all to show, as I have done, that the truth of the assumption of Mary is contained implicitly in scripture, as is implied in the mystery of her virginal motherhood.

Hope of unity

Even if the definition of the Assumption was for the moment a source of scandal, it could thus become a motive for hope.

Pius XII wrote: 'There is good reason to hope that all the faithful will be inspired with greater devotion towards their Mother in heaven, and that all those who make their boast in the name of Christ will long more fervently to be united with the Mystical Body, as their love for her, who is Mother to every member of it, grows stronger yet.'

Vatican II in turn ends its marian teaching with an invitation to pray to Mary for unity:

'The entire body of the faithful pours forth

The Lamenting of Christ. Detail. Fra Angelico.
Museum of S. Marco, Venice.

urgent supplications to the Mother of God and of men that she, who aided the beginnings of the Church with her prayers, may now, exalted as she is above the angels and saints, intercede before her Son in the fellowship of all the saints, until all families of people, whether they are honoured with the title of Christian or whether they still do not know the Saviour, may be happily gathered together in peace and harmony into one People of God, for the glory of the Most Holy and Undivided Trinity' (*Lumen Gentium*, 69).

The glory of the Holy Trinity

We should note that among the expected fruits of the proclamation of the assumption Pius XII mentioned the glory of the Holy Trinity: 'It will be for the glory of the most holy Trinity to which the Virgin Mother of God is united by quite special bonds.'

The present significance of the assumption in the setting of a materialist world

To be significant, a dogmatic definition must relate to a certain current situation which justifies it. The Church does not define a dogma to make a new dogma.

Nor does the Church have a specific function reserved to the definition of new dogmas.

However, in some cases the teaching function of the Church includes the need or at least the opportunity to define a revealed truth.

This necessity arises in cases where the Christian faith must be safeguarded against the heresies which falsify it or gravely threaten it. That is not the case with the assumption of Mary.

However, it was opportune that this dogma should have been defined for the greater good of the faithful, in the present context of a world which atheistic ideologies have made materialistic.

Atheistic materialism

Pius XII wrote: '(There is) reason, too, to hope that as men contemplate Mary's noble example,

they will understand better what value there is in a human life, if it be devoted to the doing of God's will and the service of others. The lying doctrines of materialism and the consequent decay of morals threaten even now to put out the light of conscience, and to sacrifice human lives in the service of fresh quarrels. But here is a beacon, clear to all eyes, pointing us towards the high destiny for which body and soul alike were created.'

The Church does not condemn the efforts that humanity is making in our time to improve the human condition by scientific, economic and social progress. Quite the contrary. It does not condemn matters, but denounces materialism or false conceptions of a purely human salvation reduced to the sole dimension of an earthly and temporal liberation.

In 1950 Pius XII was thinking of Marxism, from which most of the countries of Eastern Europe were to be liberated in 1990. But the world still needs to be liberated from many injustices, like many other forms of materialism.

A theology of liberation

The words of Pius XII still remain relevant today when they speak of a 'theology of liberation'. Christians must contribute on earth to the liberation of the oppressed, particularly the poorest. They must work to establish a society in which more freedom, justice and peace reign. But the salvation of humanity should not be reduced to the sole temporal dimension of a social and political liberation. Furthermore, that can only be realized in the ferment of Christian salvation and the values of the gospel.

The Church reminds us that there is no true and total liberation for humanity other than that which can be achieved eternally in the kingdom of God, to which we attain through the paschal mystery of Christ, dead and risen.

The Church again reminds us that there is no authentic and integral promotion for human beings other than that which allows them, by developing their natural, cultural and social values, to attain the full dimension of children of God in response to their divine calling.

Finally, the Church reminds us that the eternal kingdom of God is the sole ultimate end of human history and of all the temporal efforts of human beings in their earthly lives.

Consequently, at the beginning of the mass of 15 August, the feast of the Assumption, we recite this prayer: 'May we see heaven as our final goal and come to share her (Mary's) glory.

The assumption of Mary strengthens our hope in our own resurrection

Pius XII wrote: 'May faith in the bodily Assumption of our Lady teach our faith in the Resurrection to strike deeper roots, bear fruit more abundantly!'

Certainly the assumption of Mary is not the foundation of our hope in the resurrection, but only a fruit of the resurrection of Jesus, which contributes to strengthening our hope. It is the resurrection of Christ which, according to St Paul, is the pledge of our own resurrection (I Cor. 15.12–23: I Thess. 4.14).

However, this resurrection which is promised us for the end of time is already realized for Mary. It is the image of our own glory that we can already contemplate in Mary's glory.

Thanks to the mystery of the assumption of Mary, the mystery of our glorious resurrection is more present to us every year, on 15 August, when we can already celebrate the mystery of our own glory.

The Virgin. Russian fresco.

The assumption of Mary – an endorsement of the human body

In our society, some people make the human body an idol, while others scorn it. The Church, in celebrating the assumption of Mary, exalts the true dignity of the human body.

In our age, when the human body is so often outraged, humiliated, vilified and tortured, is it not comforting to see the human body attaining the pinnacle of glory?

The human person is not a pure spirit but a spiritual person. We express ourselves in bodies and enter into a relationship with other human beings through these bodies, which also have a relationship to the material universe.

The aspiration of the person to immortality does not only relate to our spiritual souls. It is a heresy to sing that we only have souls to save. Human beings cannot be integrally saved or arrive at the fullness of glory without a transfiguration of their bodies.

In preaching the resurrection of the human body and the reign of human beings over the created universe, Christianity is responding to one of the most profound human aspirations. In Mary we see how this hope will be realized for each one of us, by bringing the whole of human being to its perfection.

The assumption of Mary, the glorification of woman

The key aim of the cult of Mary is not like that of certain feminist movements, to exalt women in the church and to work to promote them by giving them the same rights and opportunities in society as men, right though this may be.

This Marian dimension of Christian life takes on special importance in relation to women and their status. In fact, feminity has a unique relationship with the Mother of the Redeemer, a subject which can be studied in greater depth elsewhere. Here I simply wish to note that the figure of Mary of Nazareth sheds light on womanhood as such by the very fact that God, in the sublime event of the Incarnation of his Son, entrusted himself to the ministry, the free and active ministry of a woman. It can thus be said that women, by looking to Mary, find in her the secret of living their femininity with dignity and of achieving their own true advancement. In the light of Mary, the Church sees in the face of women the reflection of a beauty which mirrors the loftiest sentiments of which the human heart is capable: the self-offering totality of love; the strength that is capable of bearing the greatest sorrows; limitless fidelity and tireless devotion to work; the ability to combine penetrating intuition with words of support and encouragement.

Redemptoris Mater, 46

Notre Dame
de Fonte Grâce.
Plateau d'Assy.
Mosaic by
Fernand Léger.
Photo:
Damien-Avril.

94

The veneration offered to Mary in the Church, inseparably from Christian worship offered to Christ, is bound up with the maternal role that Mary has played in the history of salvation.

However, it is a fact that the human glorification accomplished in Christ the God-Man has also been manifested down to the present day in the female being.

So the assumption of Mary can appear as that which henceforth achieves the mystery of the transfiguration of our humanity, since it is already realized not only in Christ, the New Adam, but also in the Virgin Mary, the New Eve.

John Paul II is fond of emphasizing this aspect of the assumption of Mary. He did this both in his encyclical on the mother of the Redeemer and in his apostolic letter *Mulieris dignitatem* on the dignity of the vocation of woman, on the occasion of the Marian Year which ended on 15 August 1988.

Mary, the eschatological icon of the Church

The Church will continue to remember the happy expression of Fr Bouyer:

'For us, in this assumption which is the last stage of the uninterrupted progression of grace and fidelity which was her historical existence, Mary is the original example of this victory over death that the heavenly Adam, raised as the firstborn from among the dead, wills to communicate to his many brothers, children of the earthly Adam.

Thus *par excellence* Mary is the eschatological icon of the church, the promise already realized of the ultimate realizations offered to human hopes, to the hope of faith, and which justifies its sacrifices' (*Le Culte de la mère de Dieu*, 1954).

In Mary, it is the Church which in its first member has already attained its glorious end. Mary is the type of the heavenly city, the holy city, the new Jerusalem 'adorned as a bride to greet her husband' (Rev. 21.2).

Under the inspiration of Fr Bouyer, Vatican II wrote: 'In the meantime the Mother of Jesus in the glory which she possesses in body and soul in heaven is the image and beginning of the Church as it is to be perfected in the world to come.

Likewise she shines forth on earth, until the day of the Lord shall come (cf. II Peter 3.10), a sign of certain hope and comfort to the people of God' (*Lumen Gentium*, 68).

The preface of the mass of 15 August expresses this eschatological aspect of the mystery of Mary very well: 'Today the Virgin Mother of God was taken up into heaven to be the beginning and the pattern of the Church in its perfection, and a sign of hope and comfort for your people on their pilgrim way.'

The woman of the Apocalypse

That is why the liturgy is fond of representing the Virgin Mary in terms of the woman of the Apocalypse crowned with stars. In the literal sense this woman personifies the Church. But she can also *par excellence* signify Mary as a figure of the Church to come: 'And a great portent appeared in heaven, a woman clothed with the sun, with the moon under her feet, and on her head a crown of twelve stars' (Rev. 1, the first reading for the mass of the feast of the Assumption).

6

Mary and the Diffusion of Graces

The maternal presence of Mary at Pentecost

It remains for us to consider the maternal function of Mary in the time of the Church which was inaugurated by the Holy Spirit of Pentecost. The present role of Mary in relation to grace, the personal gift of the Holy Spirit, remains identical to the role that she played at the moment of the incarnation.

At the annunciation, when the Holy Spirit came upon her (Luke 1.35), Mary welcomed in her womb the Son of God, who became incarnate in her. At Pentecost, when the Holy Spirit descended on the apostles, she was with them to implore and welcome through her own prayer the gift of the Holy Spirit: 'All these with one accord devoted themselves to prayer, together with the women and Mary the mother of Jesus' (Acts 1.14).

On this subject Vatican II writes: 'We see Mary by her prayers imploring the gift of the Spirit, who had already overshadowed her in the Annunciation' (*Lumen Gentium*, 59).

John Paul II has also evoked this maternal presence of Mary at Pentecost: Mary was present at the Pentecost in the mystery of Christ her Son. She was also present at Pentecost in the mystery of the Church which welcomes the gift of the Holy Spirit disseminated by Christ.

And so, in the redemptive economy of grace, brought about through the action of the Holy Spirit, there is a unique correspondence between the moment of the Incarnation of the Word and the moment of the birth of the Church. The person who links these two moments is Mary: Mary at Nazareth and Mary in the Upper Room at Jerusalem. In both cases her discreet yet essential presence indicates the path of 'birth from the Holy Spirit'. Thus she who is present in the mystery of Christ as Mother becomes – by the will of the Son and the power of the Holy Spirit – present in the mystery of the Church. In the Church too she continues to be a maternal presence.

Redemptoris Mater, 24

A communal doctrine, not defined

The maternal mediation of Mary at Pentecost is a communal doctrine, but one that is not defined. Today it is still the object of numerous theological discussions, above all about the forms of any contribution by Mary to the diffusion of the graces.

In what sense and in what way is Mary through her maternal intercession the mediator of all the graces?

The teaching of Vatican II

The Second Vatican Council did not want to enter into theological controversies about the mediation of Mary. However, it retained the fact of a spiritual motherhood of Mary in the economy of grace.

It avoided using the term *mediatrix*, which could have led to misunderstandings. But it did not do away completely with this title of Mary *mediatrix*, provided that the maternal mediation of Mary before Christ is given a quite different nature from the sole priestly mediation of Christ, the one mediator with the Father.

'This motherhood of Mary in the order of grace continues uninterruptedly from the consent which she loyally gave at the Annunciation and which she sustained without wavering beneath the cross, until the eternal fulfilment of all the elect. Taken up to heaven she did not lay aside this saving office but by her manifold intercession continues to bring us the gifts of eternal salvation.

By her maternal charity, she cares for the brethren of her Son, who still journey on earth surrounded by dangers and difficulties, until they are led into their blessed home. Therefore the Blessed Virgin is invoked in the Church under the titles of Advocate, Helper, Benefactress, and Mediatrix. This, however, is so understood that it neither takes away anything from nor adds anything to the dignity and efficacy of Christ the one Mediator' (*Lumen Gentium*, 62; Vatican II here retains the title Mediatrix, referring in a note to the encyclicals of Leo XIII, Pius X, Pius XI, and Pius XII's radio broadcast of 13 May 1946).

The spiritual motherhood of Mary:
Mary, mother of the Church

According to St Thomas Aquinas' well-known expression, the humanity of Christ remains 'the conjoint instrument of his divinity'.

Jesus has earned us grace by his humanity. Even in our day it is by the mediation of his human nature that he gives us the grace of divine life.

Now this humanity of the Saviour comes to him from Mary. So Christ effectively produces grace in each of our souls by the mediation of a humanity given to him by Mary.

As mother of Christ who gives grace, in this way Mary is mother of all grace. By bringing to birth the Christ who is the author of all grace, she has brought us all to birth to the life of grace.

As Vatican II writes, 'In a wholly singular way Mary co-operated by her obedience, faith, hope and burning charity in the work of the Saviour in restoring supernatural life to souls' (*Lumen Gentium*, 61).

Spiritual motherhood from the incarnation on

We must never lose sight of the fact that this spiritual motherhood of Mary in respect of us remains entirely based on her motherhood in respect of Christ, her son according to the flesh.

It was at the incarnation that Mary became our mother. She could not remain mother of God according to the flesh without becoming spiritually the mother of all human beings.

The Son of God became incarnate in Mary as the head of humanity, so that she should represent his body, the Church, in its fullness. It is

Our Lady of Hope. Detail. Cathedral of Our Lady, Dijon. Eleventh century.

impossible to separate the head and the members of this body. The Virgin Mary is the mother of the whole Christ. She cannot be mother of the Saviour without being mother of all the saved. She cannot be the mother of Christ without becoming the mother of all Christians. By her maternal, physical, relationship to Christ the Head, Mary is *par excellence* in a spiritual maternal relationship to all the members of the body of the Church.

Vatican II takes up a remark of St Augustine (*De sancta virginitate* 6): 'Mary is truly mother of the members [of Christ] . . . because she co-operated by her charity in the birth, in the Church, of the faithful who are members of this Head' (*Lumen Gentium*, 62).

And later on the council is more specific: 'The Son whom she brought forth is he whom God placed as the first born among many brethren (Rom. 8.29), that is, the faithful, in whose generation and formation she co-operates with a mother's love' (*Lumen Gentium*, 63).

The proclamation by Jesus on the cross

As both Vatican II and John Paul II recall, it is beyond question that as Jesus was dying on the cross, he gave Mary as mother to the beloved disciple, when he showed St John to Mary and said, 'Woman, behold your son', and then to St John, showing Mary to him, 'Behold your mother' (John 19.26–27: *Lumen Gentium*, 58b, and *Redemptoris Mater*, 23).

The spiritual motherhood of Mary that Jesus proclaimed on the cross was already realized in principle at the moment of the incarnation. Jesus made this very proclamation at the moment when Mary, at the foot of the cross, was fulfilling her maternal mission, repeating in the suffering of her compassion the mother's 'yes' which she pronounced in joy on the day of the annunciation.

Even if Jesus had not proclaimed it from the cross, the spiritual motherhood of Mary towards us would be implicitly confirmed in two affirmations, namely that Mary is the mother of Christ and we are the members of Christ.

Undoubtedly, we find here (Mary being entrusted to John by Jesus) an expression of the Son's particular solicitude for his Mother, whom he is leaving in such great sorrow. And yet the 'testament of Christ's Cross' says more. Jesus highlights a new relationship between Mother and Son, the whole truth and reality of which he solemnly confirms. One can say that if Mary's motherhood of the human race had already been outlined, now it is clearly stated and established. It emerges from the definitive accomplishment of the Redeemer's Paschal Mystery. The Mother of Christ, who stands at the very centre of this mystery – a mystery which embraces each individual and all humanity – is given as mother to every single individual and all mankind. The man at the foot of the Cross is John, 'the disciple whom he loved'. But it is not he alone. Following tradition the Council does not hesitate to call Mary 'the Mother of Christ and mother of mankind' . . . Indeed she is 'clearly the mother of the members of Christ . . . since she cooperated out of love so that there might be born in the Church the faithful'.

Redemptoris Mater, 23

'Mother of the Church'

We are to understand in the same way the title 'Mother of the Church' with which Paul VI hailed Mary in his Discourse of 21 November 1964, following on from the Dogmatic Constitution on the Church. As John Paul II later commented:

'At the Council Paul VI solemnly proclaimed that Mary is the Mother of the Church, "that is, Mother of the entire Christian people, both faithful and pastors". Later, in 1968, in the Profession of Faith known as the "Credo of the People of God", he restated this truth in an even more forceful way in these words: "We believe that the Most Holy Mother of God, the new Eve, the Mother of the Church, carries on in heaven her maternal role with regard to the members of Christ, cooperating in the birth and development of divine life in the souls of the redeemed"' (*Redemptoris Mater*, 47).

The intercession of Mary as mother and queen

Mary is 'mother of grace' not only in the sense that she brought forth the God-Man who is the author of grace, but also in the sense that all grace given by Jesus receives the motherly imprint of Mary's intercession.

The Virgin Mary, while not the redeemer and mediator between us and the Father, intercedes for us as a mother with her Son, bringing to bear in her prayer the motherly consent which she has not ceased to give to the work of redemption since the incarnation.

Having arrived since her assumption at the glory of the resurrection, Mary can know us all, maintain a personal relationship with all, and by her maternal intercession obtain for us the graces which her Son gives us.

Vatican II writes: 'Taken up to heaven, . . . by her manifold intercession Mary continues to bring us the gifts of eternal salvation (*Lumen Gentium*, 62).

The same intercession as at Cana

Thus Mary continues to exercise the role of maternal intercession which she already exer-cised at the marriage feast of Cana: 'Moved with pity, she brought about by her intercession the beginning of miracles of Jesus the Messiah (John 2.1–11)' (*Lumen Gentium*, 58).

Mary as queen

The church invokes Mary most often as queen, to express the universal character of her spiritual motherhood of the Church.

This title of queen, which goes back to the Fathers, was proclaimed solemnly by Pius XII in the encyclical *Ad Caeli Reginam* of 11 October 1954

> With a heart that is truly a mother's does she approach the problem of our salvation, and is solicitous for the whole human race; made Queen of heaven and earth by the Lord, exalted above all choirs of angels and saints, and standing at the right hand of her only Son, Jesus Christ our Lord, she intercedes powerfully for us with a mother's prayers, obtains what she seeks, and cannot be refused.
>
> *Ad Caeli Reginam*, 42

Mary is present at Cana in Galilee as the Mother of Jesus, and in a significant way she contributes to that 'beginning of the signs' which reveal the messianic power of her Son. We read: 'When the wine gave out, the mother of Jesus said to him, "They have no wine". And Jesus said to her, "O woman, what have you to do with me? My hour has not yet come"' (John 2.3–4). In John's Gospel that 'hour' means the time appointed by the Father when the Son accomplishes his task and is to be glorified (cf. John 7.30; 8.20; 12.23, 27; 13.1; 17.1; 19.27). Even though Jesus' reply to his mother sounds like a refusal . . . Mary nevertheless turns to the servants and says to them: 'Do whatever he tells you' (John 2.5). Then Jesus orders the servants to fill the stone jars with water, and the water becomes wine, better than the wine which has previously been served to the wedding guests . . .

. . . The description of the Cana event outlines what is actually manifested as a new kind of motherhood according to the spirit and not just according to the flesh, that is to say Mary's solicitude for human beings, her coming to them in the wide variety of their wants and needs. At Cana in Galilee there is shown only one concrete aspect of human need, apparently a small one and of little importance ('They have no wine'). But it has a symbolic value: this coming to the aid of human needs means, at the same time, bringing those needs within the radius of Christ's messianic mission and salvific power. Thus there is a mediation: Mary . . . acts as a mediatrix not as an outsider, but in her position as mother. She knows that as such she can point out to her Son the needs of mankind, and in fact, she 'has the right' to do so. Her mediation is thus in the nature of intercession: Mary 'intercedes' for mankind . . .

Another essential element of Mary's maternal task is found in her words to the servants: 'Do whatever he tells you'. The Mother of Christ presents herself as the spokeswoman of her Son's will, pointing out those things which must be done so that the salvific power of the Messiah may be manifested. At Cana, thanks to the intercession of Mary and the obedience of the servants, Jesus begins 'his hour'. At Cana Mary appears as believing in Jesus. Her faith evokes his first 'sign' and helps to kindle the faith of the disciples.

Redemptoris Mater, 21

when he instituted the feast of the Queenship of Mary.

This feast, first fixed by Pius XII on 31 May, was then moved to the octave of the feast of the Assumption, 22 August.

The difference between the intercession of Christ and that of Mary

This intercession of the Virgin is distinct from that of Christ, and is practised in a very different way.

The priestly prayer of Christ, the unique intercessor with the Father, derives its power from his redeeming merit. It is the formulation of a real right to justify us by the grace which he has obtained for us on the cross.

The motherly prayer of Mary, who intercedes for us with Christ, is not the expression of a will claiming its due. It is the expression of a desire which attracts, or rather welcomes, the grace of Christ by entrusting itself and abandoning itself totally to his good will, as Mary did at Cana.

So Mary's prayer, based on her maternal 'yes', cannot have any force other than that which is proper to the prayer of all human creatures redeemed by Christ. But the prayer of the mother of Christ the Redeemer has this force of intercession in its fullness. It is as efficacious as the prayer of a member of the ransomed church can be, and its power, in this order that it does not go beyond, is total. The Church denotes this efficacy when it speaks of the almighty supplication of Mary.

That is why the Church which prays to Christ, the sole intercessor with the Father and the sole source of all the graces, also addresses itself to the Virgin Mary its mother, asking her to intercede with him and 'obtain for us the graces of salvation' (*Lumen Gentium*, 58).

The Virgin of Pity. Detail. Enguerrand Quarton. 1452.
Condé Museum, Chantilly.

The motherly mediation of Mary who acts in the ecclesial communion with all the saints

Mary, a type of the Church as 'communion of saints'

To understand the maternal role of Mary in the diffusion of all the graces, as at the moment of the incarnation and at the foot of the cross, we have to envisage her in her ecclesial dimension.

Mary, as mother of Christ, is also, as I have said, the type of the church. Mary is in the church. Having already attained the glory of the resurrection she nevertheless continues to live and act in the communion of the whole church of which she is the first member.

'In union with the whole Church we honour Mary, the ever-virgin mother of Jesus Christ our Lord and God', we say in the first eucharistic prayer. We should make it clear that Mary is not a type of the Church considered under the aspect of its ministerial hierarchy – pope, bishops and priests – but is the figure of the church constituted in communion with the saints who live in union with Christ.

As Vatican II says, 'The mother of God is a type of the Church in the order of faith, charity, and perfect union with Christ' (*Lumen Gentium*, 63; cf. 53).

Mary is a type of the Church, which is a community of believers, those who in order to benefit from the grace of Christ must receive it through acts of faith, that active faith which St Paul says is a condition of justification.

The Church continues to welcome salvation by faith with Mary and in communion with her. It is always in this communion that the Church disposes itself to receive the grace of Christ and welcomes this as the personal gift of the Holy Spirit.

The need for a good disposition to receive grace

We must never forget that while all grace is effectively given us by the Spirit, we receive this grace of divine life fruitfully only if we are ready to welcome it.

Far from remaining passive, the person sanctified by Christ must co-operate personally in his work of grace by acts of virtue and by a life in conformity with the gospel.

Adults who have not been baptized can, and even must, under the action of the first actual grace, prepare themselves to receive the sanctifying grace of justification. God always takes the first step: God takes the initiative in our sanctification. But we must respond freely to the call of God by accepting the gift of his grace and by making ourselves worthy to receive it. Grace never constrains human wills. It works efficaciously in its nature only if it finds the necessary dispositions there, after already evoking them. The sacraments, even administered in a valid way, can lack efficacy if there is insufficient disposition in the subject who receives them.

God even wants us to be disposed to receive his grace by asking for it in prayer: 'Ask, and it will be given you . . . the heavenly Father will give the Holy Spirit to those who ask him' (Luke 11.9–13).

God certainly does not need our prayers, but he treats us as free individuals. That is why he can want to bind his gifts to our prayer. As St Augustine said: 'God does not require our prayer to make our desires known to him, but so that we can welcome what he is preparing to give us.'

The solidarity of Christians united in the communion of saints

Now as far as this active receptivity to grace is concerned, all redeemed Christians are in solidarity with one another. There is a kind of reversibility of merits and exchange of spiritual benefits between the members of the Church. This is what is called the communion of saints.

We can pray for each other and earn merits for one another. We can help one another to receive the Lord and the gift of his grace, the personal gift of the Holy Spirit. By his apostolate, his example, his prayer and the merit of his good actions, the Christian who lives in communion with Christ can obtain from him graces of aid which will help another person to be more open to the love of the Lord.

St Paul did not cease to pray for his disciples, asking God that they should arrive at the full knowledge of his will with a perfect wisdom and true spiritual understanding (Col. 1.9). He even said, resorting to excessive language, that he would have been willing to be anathema and separated from Christ for the good of his Jewish brothers, those of his race according to the flesh (Rom. 9.3).

How many sinners have rediscovered the way of salvation thanks to the prayers and merits of the saints! Was not the conversion of St Augustine obtained by the tears and supplications of his mother St Monica?

Did not Jesus himself ask his disciples to pray that the name of the Father should be glorified, that his kingdom should come and his will be done (Matt. 6.9–10)?

Virtuous acts and the prayers of the righteous can thus be dedicated to God in order to supplement or strengthen the dispositions by which the sinner can co-operate with grace.

Let us remember the man condemned to death who showed a sign of repentance and accepted Christ's forgiveness only at the moment when he found himself on the scaffold. This conversion *in extremis*, obtained through the fervent prayer of the little Thérèse of Lisieux, provides a signi-ficant example. When it comes to free receptivity to grace, we are all more or less mediators for one another before Christ, our one mediator with the Father.

All together we form a spiritual community which is bound to the Father through Christ the mediator. We are redeemed and sanctified by being in solidarity with Christ, the divine Word, who by his incarnation has taken all humanity in charge.

However, as I said, this mediation of Christ requires of humanity a free commitment to his paschal mystery and a voluntary welcoming of his redemptive grace.

In this co-operation with the sanctifying grace of Christ our head, we are all, as members of his body the Church, in solidarity with one another. The refusals of some and the consents of others take place through the human community.

That is why, despite the incomparable power of the prayer of Christ, we also have need of the prayer of the saints. Also, even at mass, we offer the sacrifice of Jesus, which is of infinite value, in communion with all the saints whose memory we evoke in the eucharistic prayer.

The motherly mediation of Mary of the same nature as the mediation of all the saints

While 'in union with the whole Church we honour Mary, the ever-virgin mother of Jesus Christ our Lord and God' (as is said in the first eucharistic prayer), the intercession of Mary, from whom we implore help to obtain the grace of the Lord, is of the same nature as the prayer of all the other saints.

As Vatican II puts it: 'The entire body of the faithful . . . prays to Mary to intercede before her son in the fellowship of all the saints . . .' (*Lumen Gentium*, 69).

This intercessory mediation of Mary in obtaining graces is of the same order as that of all the other saints. Like them, and with even greater reason because she is mother of Christ, Mary can obtain numerous graces for us: in particular the graces of a disposition to welcome the salvation offered by her Son.

Mediation realized in the best way

But Mary accomplishes this intercessory mediation, proper to all the saints who are members of the Church, in the first and best way, and attains a dimension which is personal to her.

This is first because, as I have said, as mother of Christ Mary has a power of intercession with him that no other Christian can exercise.

But this is also because, unlike the mediation of other saints, which is particular and limited, that of Mary is universal, to the point that no grace accorded by Christ is alien to her.

This mediation of Mary in all the graces is, as I have said, the object of a communal doctrine taught by many popes. It is not defined as a dogma of faith, and the way in which it is exercised remains very much a matter of discussion.

Without going into theological controversies we can note one certain fact: the Virgin Mary is the only member of the redeemed Church who consented to the paschal sacrifice, the source of all the graces. So by this same acquiescence, renewed in her perpetual heavenly intercession, she continues to co-operate in the diffusion of all the graces by Christ.

Karl Rahner strongly emphasized this eternal 'yes' of Mary's.

Universal intercession and universal communion with all the members of humanity were accorded to Mary by virtue of her glorious assumption. The resurrection of her body makes Mary present to all human beings and to all the universe.

This universality is the difference between the motherly mediation of Mary and the mediation or intercession of all the other saints. In communion with all the saints, Mary is the first, and her intercession has a universal scope.

Through Mary and in communion with her we have all acquiesced in the redemptive sacrifice of Calvary: today again, in communion with Mary, we say 'yes' to each grace offered by Christ, even if we are not always aware that we do.

Mary's prayer and motherly consent strengthen our prayer and our own 'yes'

Thus the prayer of Mary strengthens our prayer, and her commitment to the universal work of salvation strengthens our personal commitment, of disposition and welcome, to each particular grace. At least Mary obtains for us graces of disposition, since all grace, even that of simple disposition, comes from Christ, the source of all the graces.

Each time that we welcome the grace of Christ we personally renew the 'yes' pronounced by Mary in our name to all, at the annunciation and then on Calvary. Just as at one time, in Mary and by Mary, we welcomed Christ at the moment of the incarnation, so again today, again in communion with her, we welcome all grace and dispose ourselves to receive it.

As Fr Bouyer wrote: 'Only Christ gives us grace, because only he is God made man. But we do not receive grace without ourselves and our own free commitment. And this commitment of humanity to the gift of God realized in the humanity of the Son of God comes about in each of us only through imitation of and dependence upon what was done in the Virgin. It is in this sense that Mary is called mediatrix of all the graces . . . Understood in this way, I believe that this mediation, if one wants to give it that name, admirably sums up the very basis of the attitude of the Church and Catholic Christians to Mary. They live in a filial dependence on her, as children dependent on their mother' (*Le Culte de la mère de Dieu*, 1954).

The same motherly role for Mary as at the incarnation

We see how the presant role of Mary in grace remains in the same line as, or rather as a sequel and extension to, the gift of all grace, the motherly role that she played at the incarnation.

Mary is 'mother of grace' because she has made us be born to the life of grace by engendering the one who is the author of this life. But she is also 'mother of grace' for a second reason: being the first to welcome Christ, the source of all blessings, by her faith, she continues to be the one who opens us up to all grace.

It is always in communion with Mary, even if sometimes we may not be aware of it, that we welcome the grace of Christ, the one mediator with the Father.

Mary, the help of Christians

Consequently, the more sinful we are, the more we are closed to grace by our hardness, our feebleness, our faithlessness or our indifference, the more need we have of Mary, 'the help of Christians', to remedy the inadequacies of our dispositions.

The grace of Christ never fails us, but our dispositions, our availability, our openness can be insufficient. Mary's own role is to obtain for us graces of dispositions and welcome, since she was always totally available, through her maternal consent and the obedience of her faith, to the work of salvation realized by Jesus.

By her maternal intercession, Mary communicates her own 'yes' to us so that it welcomes the grace of Christ in us, just as formerly her consent welcomed the divine Word when he became incarnate in her womb, to be born to humankind.

This universal mediation of Mary in the communion of all the saints does not in any way prevent us from also having recourse to other saints. We can never have too many intercessors to strengthen our prayer. And every saint, by the particular quality of his or her holiness, can help us to practise more specially one or other virtue of Christian holiness.

This mediation of other saints, far from excluding that of Mary, in fact presupposes it. Among the saints, Mary is the first member of the holy Church. In fact the personal commitment of each saint to the saving will of the Lord is included in the 'yes' pronounced by Mary at the time of the incarnation in the name of the whole Church of the saints. The mediation of the saints, of each member of the holy Church, is exercised in imitation of and in dependence on the universal mediation of Mary.

Benedict XV recalled this at the time of the approval of the two miracles which were attributed to the intercession of Joan of Arc, since they had taken place at Lourdes. He remarked: 'We must never exclude the memory of Mary, even when a miracle seems to have to be attributed to the intercession or mediation of a blessed one or a saint.'

The significance of devotion to Mary

All that already helps us to understand the significance of the devotion to Mary that has always been a spontaneous part of the Christian life.

As Vatican II writes: 'From the earliest times . . . the faithful have taken refuge together in her protection in all their perils and needs' (*Lumen Gentium*, 66).

Charles Péguy confessed that he could not say the Our Father but could nevertheless recite the Hail Mary.

It is in you, our patron and mediator before the God whose mother you are, that the human race puts all its joy. It awaits your protection; in you alone it finds refuge, and by you alone it hopes to be defended. I too come to you with a fervent soul, since I do not have the courage to approach your Son, and I beg your intercession to obtain my salvation. All-compassionate one, you who are the mother of the God of mercy, have pity on your servant!

St Ephraem, *Prayer to Mary*, fourth century

'There is something very right about this,' wrote Cardinal Daniélou. 'When one cannot say the Our Father because one is not worthy, if one does not have a filial disposition, in grace, it nevertheless seems to be that one can say Hail Mary because there is a presence of Mary where Jesus and grace are not yet present. That is why there is a mysterious relationship between Mary and sinners; it is this that is felt so much by sinners who pray to Mary when they cannot yet pray to Jesus, or can no longer do so because of their infidelities' (Le Mystère de l'Avent).

One day Paul Claudel replied to a Jesuit father who asked him why he was praying before a statue of the Virgin and not before the altar of the blessed sacrament, 'I am preparing with Mary to go to find her divine Son.'

Isn't that also the significance of our rosary? In reciting the Hail Mary we evoke before God the Father the scene of the annunciation; in order that God shall hear us we want to have the free consent that Mary gave in our name to all at the incarnation of her son. In some way we come under Mary's 'yes' so that it welcomes in us the divine grace, as once it opened humankind to the coming of the divine Word when he became incarnate.

The recitation of the Angelus, which also evokes the free consent of the incarnation of the Word in Mary at the moment of the annunciation, is equally one of the practices of marian devotion most commended by the Church. In the next chapter we shall be returning (p. 113) to the significance of devotion to Mary and the cult of Mary among Christian people.

Mary and the Christian apostolate

We can also understand better the significance of our recourse to Mary in our apostolic activities.

The apostle knows that he does not convert people and communicate grace to them himself. It is the role of Christ who sends the gift of the Holy Spirit and precedes the apostles wherever they go to evangelize.

However, the aim of our apostolic activities is to prepare people to recognize Christ and welcome his grace, by trying to create in them and in their sphere of life favourable conditions for welcoming the gospel and for the sanctifying action of the Holy Spirit.

Since Mary is precisely this privileged milieu where, since the incarnation of the Word and up to Pentecost, the divine work of salvation has been in operation in humanity, it is good to have recourse to the help of Mary in order to assure the efficacy of our apostolate, above all at difficult times. As Vatican II says: 'The Church, in her apostolic work too, rightly looks to her who gave birth to Christ, in order that through the Church he can be born and increase in the hearts of the faithful . . .' (Lumen Gentium, 65).

The significance of liturgical invocations

'Pray for us, holy mother of God, that we may be worthy of the promises of Jesus Christ.' That is how we ask Mary to obtain for us the dispositional graces to make us worthy of the promises of Jesus Christ; that is, which prepare us to benefit from the salvation attained by Christ.

Mary does not redeem us; she does not sanctify us as Christ does, but she is the praying Virgin, the Virgin who says 'yes', the welcoming Virgin, the Virgin who is actively receptive to redemption. Mary helps us to become receptive, to open us to the gift of grace that Christ offers us, by obtaining specially through her intercession graces of good dispositions for us.

The opening prayer of the mass of 1 January, for the feast of Mary, Mother of God sufficiently sums up all our theology of marian mediation:

'God our Father
may we always profit by the prayers
of the Virgin Mother Mary,
for you bring us life and salvation
through Jesus Christ her Son
who lives and reigns with you and the Holy Spirit,
one God, for ever and ever.'

Pentecost. Detail. Manuscript by the
monks of Helmarshausen. Twelfth century.

The Church knows and teaches with Saint Paul that there is only one mediator (I Tim. 2.5–6). 'The maternal role of Mary towards people in no way obscures or diminishes the unique mediation of Christ, but rather shows its power' (*Lumen Gentium*, 60) . . .

In effect, Mary's mediation is intimately linked with her motherhood. It possesses a specifically maternal character . . . (Mary's role) flows from her divine motherhood and can be understood and lived in faith only on the basis of the full truth of this motherhood. Since by virtue of divine election Mary is the earthly Mother of the Father's consubstantial Son and his 'generous companion' in the work of redemption, 'she is a mother to us in the order of grace' (*Lumen Gentium*, 61). This role constitutes a real dimension of her presence in the saving mystery of Christ and the Church . . .

Mary's motherhood, completely pervaded by her spousal attitude as the 'handmaid of the Lord', constitutes the first and fundamental dimension of that mediation which the Church confesses and proclaims in her regard' (*Lumen Gentium*, 62) . . . This basic fact of being the Mother of the Son of God is from the very beginning a complete openness to the person of Christ, to his whole work, to his whole mission . . .

After her Son's departure, her motherhood remains in the Church as maternal mediation: interceding for all her children, the Mother cooperates in the saving work of her Son, the Redeemer of the world. In fact the Council teaches that the 'motherhood of Mary in the order of grace . . . will last without interruption until the eternal fulfilment of all the elect' (*Lumen Gentium*, 62).

'For', the text goes on, 'taken up to heaven, she did not lay aside this saving role, but by her manifold acts of intercession continues to win for us gifts of eternal salvation' (*Lumen Gentium*, 62). With this character of 'intercession', first manifested at Cana in Galilee, Mary's mediation continues in the history of the Church and the world. We read that Mary 'by her maternal charity, cares for the brethren of her Son who still journey on earth surrounded by dangers and difficulties, until they are led to their happy homeland' (*Lumen Gentium*, 62). In this way Mary's motherhood continues unceasingly in the Church as mediation which intercedes, and the Church expresses her faith in this truth by invoking Mary 'under the titles of Advocate, Auxiliatrix, Adjutrix and Mediatrix' (*Lumen Gentium*, 62).

Redemptoris Mater, 38–40

So Christ is our one mediator with the Father, but Mary, through her motherhood, is our mediatrix with Christ in the welcome that we reserve for the Lord.

Mary's maternal mediation is different from the priestly mediation of Christ

Throughout the third part of his marian encyclical, John Paul II deals with the 'maternal mediation of Mary'.

That is what he calls it, constantly referring to the teaching of Vatican II. The Council avoided the title *mediatrix*, without excluding it, but firmly emphasized the maternal function of Mary in the actual obtaining of grace.

So I shall not hesitate to follow John Paul II in speaking of the mediation of Mary, if it is understood in this specifically maternal sense.

The motherly mediation of Mary is quite different from the priestly mediation of Christ, to which moreover it is always firmly subordinated. The motherly mediation of Mary is not a complement to that of Christ, nor is it an extension of it.

The Virgin Mary must not be represented in a vertical hierarchy as a second mediator who interposes herself between Christ and us to extend the mediation that Christ exercises between God the Father and humankind. As Vatican II says, 'Mary's function in no way obscures or diminishes the unique mediation of Christ, but rather shows its power' (*Lumen Gentium*, 60).

Coronation of the Virgin. Detail. Enguerrand Quarton. Museum of Villeneuse-les-Avignon.

Christ the Head is in direct contact with all the members of his mystical body, and if the Virgin is the first member of it, she does not separate the others from Christ. So we cannot suppose that the grace of divine life which flows from Christ, the sole living source, must first pass through Mary before arriving at us (John 7.38).

All grace flows directly from the fullness of grace possessed by Jesus in his humanity. This grace of Jesus is called 'capital grace', that is, the grace of Christ the Head who makes all the members of his body, the church, participate in his own grace.

That is why I do not like the image of the neck or the channel which have been used to represent Mary's mediation. Mary is indeed the first member of the Church. But in the mystical body of the Church she is not like the neck which separates the head from the other members. Nor is Mary a channel through which the grace of Christ flows before coming into us.

Nor do I like the comparison of the role of Mary in the diffusion of graces with the instrumental role of the sacraments. The sacraments are instrumental causes of grace because they make present in signs the words and actions of Christ, who sanctifies us by the sacramental mediation of his humanity.

But Mary does not represent Christ in a ministerial and sacramental fashion. Moreover, her role does not lie in the sphere of the priestly action of Christ, who sanctifies us through the mediation of his humanity. It is exercised in the Church which, as the communion of saints, must be open to the grace of salvation.

Nor again do I like the titles sometimes attributed to Mary of treasury and distributor of graces. Some preachers have even imagined the mediation of Mary and justified its necessity by saying that Jesus entrusted to his mother the totality of graces that he merited by his cross, for her to distribute as she thought fit to all those who resort to her. This invention is not only in bad taste: it gives an erroneous idea of the mediation of Mary.

So Mary does not act on the same level as Christ, who brings salvation and gives us grace. As Vatican II writes, 'No creature could ever be counted along with the Incarnate Word and Redeemer' (*Lumen Gentium*, 62).

However, Mary acts in the Church, which receives salvation and welcomes it with faith, by a free consent of active receptivity.

Always a role of consent

Without going into current controversies on the co-operation of Mary in our salvation, Vatican II has retained above all the idea of a role of consent: 'This motherhood of Mary in the order of grace continues uninterruptedly from the consent which she loyally gave at the Annunciation and which she sustained without wavering beneath the cross, until the eternal fulfilment of all the elect' (*Lumen Gentium*, 62).

We prepare with Mary to welcome the glorious Christ of the parousia

'Lord Jesus, come in glory,' we say in the acclamation which follows the eucharistic consecration.

In this time of the Church on its way to the parousia of the Lord, still today it is in Mary, with Mary, the type of the church, that the church gathers as a single 'spouse' to prepare to welcome her bridegroom for the eternal nuptials.

In the advent time of the Old Testament it was in Mary, in communion with Mary, that humanity prepared to welcome the Son of God when he became incarnate for his advent.

Today still the Church continues, in communion with Mary, to prepare itself to welcome Jesus, who, at his return in glory, will definitively establish his glorious kingdom and make us participate in his reign over the world, a reign in which Mary already participates by reason of her glorious assumption.

The Church, throughout her life, maintains with the Mother of God a link which embraces, in the saving mystery, the past, the present and the future . . .

It is precisely the special bond beween humanity and this Mother which has led me to proclaim a Marian Year in the Church, in this period before the end of the Second Millennium since Christ's birth . . .

. . . Following the line of the Second Vatican Council, I wish to emphasize the special presence of the Mother of God in the mystery of Christ and his Church . . .

For it is a question not only of recalling that Mary 'preceded' the entry of Christ the Lord into the history of the human family, but also of emphasizing, in the light of Mary, that from the moment when the mystery of the Incarnation was accomplished human history entered 'the fullness of time', and that the Church is the sign of this fullness. As the People of God, the Church makes her pilgrim way towards eternity through faith, in the midst of all the peoples and nations, beginning from the day of Pentecost. Christ's Mother, who was present at the beginning of 'the time of the Church', when in expectation of the coming of the Holy Spirit she devoted herself to prayer in the midst of the Apostles and her Son's disciples, constantly 'precedes' the Church in her journey through human history. He is also the one who, precisely as the 'handmaid of the Lord', cooperates unceasingly with the work of salvation accomplished by Christ, her son.

Thus by means of this Marian Year the Church is called not only to remember everything in her past that testifies to the special maternal cooperation of the Mother of God in the work of salvation in Christ the Lord, but also, on her own part, to prepare for the future the paths of this cooperation. For the end of the Second Christian Millennium opens up as a new prospect.

Redemptoris Mater, 47–49

The Church with Mary prepares to celebrate the year 2000

It is in the perspective of this expectation of the coming of Christ that John Paul II wants us to prepare to celebrate Christmas 2000.

He wants to make the few years which separate us from the second millennium of the birth of Christ a kind of liturgical advent lived with Mary. To inaugurate this marian advent John Paul decreed a Marian Year which we celebrated from 7 June 1987 (the feast of Pentecost) to 15 August 1988 (the feast of the Assumption).

That brings us to the end of this chapter on the maternal mediation of Mary in the diffusion of graces. It is always with Mary that we say 'yes' to Christ the Redeemer and in communion with her that we welcome the grace of salvation.

Mary is the 'yes' of redeemed humanity. We proclaim that when we say that Mary is our mediatrix before Christ, the one mediator before the Father.

Mary's maternal mediation does not make a second mediation alongside the priestly mediation of Christ because it is not that participation in the mediation of Christ which alone redeems and sanctifies us. The maternal mediation of Mary is on the level of dispositional causality: it makes men and women receptive, redeemed men and women who must commit themselves freely to their salvation and co-operate actively in grace by prayer and faith.

So let us be persuaded that we always need the maternal mediation of Mary to welcome all grace, as we needed it to welcome the Son of God at the time of his incarnation and to consent to his redemptive sacrifice on Calvary.

7

The Cult of Mary and Appearances of Mary

The historical evolution and doctrinal justification of the cult of Mary

The dignity of Mother of God and the fullness of graces which result from that led to a special cult of Mary in the Church.

This cult of Mary is inferior to the cult of adoration, called *latria*, which belongs only to God; however, it is superior to the cult of veneration, called *dulia*, which is offered to the angels and the saints. That is why it is called the cult of *hyperdulia*.

The cult of Mary is not idolatry

Protestants misunderstand when they denounce this marian cult as idolatry, since Catholics do not worship the Holy Virgin. The cult that we offer to the mother of God does not give her divine status, but attests the glory which the Son of God made her reflect after his incarnation. Though this glory of Mary surpasses that of all the saints by reason of her motherhood, it is not different from the glory to which all the members of the Church are called (Rom. 8.18; II Cor. 4.17). It is already the final glory of the whole Church that we venerate in Mary, mother of Christ and type of the Church.

An integral part of Christian worship

The cult of Mary is not a special cult distinct from Christian worship.

In his apostolic exhortation on the cult of Mary Paul VI emphasized in his introduction: 'This devotion (to the Blessed Virgin Mary) fits into the only worship that is rightly called "Christian", because it takes its origin and effectiveness from Christ, finds its complete expression in Christ and leads through Christ in the Spirit to the Father'. And he returns to this at the end: 'We have dealt at length with an integral element of Christian worship' (*Marialis Cultus*, 58).

The scriptural foundations of the cult of Mary

While Holy Scripture does not speak of a cult of Mary on the part of the earliest Church, it does provide the foundations for the cult of Mary which was to arise later.

Thus we find the scriptural foundations of the cult of Mary in the respectful salutation of the angel: 'Rejoice, you who are highly favoured, the

The Visitation. Catalan. Twelfth century.

Lord is with you' (Luke 1.28). The praise of Elizabeth, filled with the Holy Spirit, reinforces this: 'You are blessed above women, and blessed too is the fruit of your womb' (Luke 1.42). The salutation and the praise of Elizabeth form the first part of the Hail Mary: 'Hail Mary, full of grace, the Lord is with you, blessed are you among all women and blessed is the fruit of your womb.' Finally, the firm foundation of the cult of Mary may be confirmed by the prophetic words of Mary herself in her Magnificat: 'From henceforth all generations shall call me blessed, for he that is mighty has magnified me' (Luke 1.48–49).

Historical evolution

From the third century, the cult of Mary developed in close connection with the worship of Christ.

At this period the Gospels were read at Christmas, and Mary appears in them. Several churches before or after Christmas commemorated Mary by reading the account of the annunciation during the ceremony.

In the fourth century the hymns of St Ephraem (who died in 373) on the birth of the Lord are also hymns of praise to his virgin mother.

St Gregory of Nazianzus (who died around 390) attests the cult of Mary, at least as private devotion. He reports that the Christian virgin Justina, at the moment when her virginity had been threatened, 'had prayed to the Virgin Mary to come to the aid of a threatened virgin' (*Discourses*, XXIV, 11).

St Epiphanius (who died in 403) teaches against the sect of the Collyridians who offered Mary idolatrous worship that 'Mary must be honoured. But the Father, the Son and the Holy Spirit must be adored; no one must adore Mary' (*Panarion* LXXIX, 7).

So the veneration of Mary entered into the cycle of festivals of saints. However, it only appeared there after the martyrs, the anniversary of whose deaths were celebrated from the second century on.

It was only in the fifth century, after the first festivals of the confessors of the faith, that the feast of the Dormition or Assumption of Mary was instituted. Other marian festivals followed, like those of the nativity and the presentation in the temple, in the seventh and eighth centuries.

So the cult of Mary might seem to be quite late. However, since the cult of goddesses was widespread in pagan society, the delay in the cult of Mary can be explained by a concern to avoid the Christian people making Mary a new goddess. Furthermore the cult of Mary could only develop after the recognition of her dignity as mother of God, which happened at the Council of Ephesus in 431.

The prayer *Sub tuum praesidium*, discovered on a papyrus in 1938, would date from this period. The term *theotokos*, 'mother of God', already appears in it. The prayer is reflected almost word for word in the Roman rite.

From the beginning of the Middle Ages, the cult of Mary attains its full development.

The *Regina caeli* appeared at the end of the tenth century.

The *Salve regina*, *Alma redemptoris* and *Ave maris stella* come from the eleventh century. The *Tota pulchra es* dates from the fourteenth century.

Protestant reactions

The development of the cult of Mary then became so excessively exuberant in the sixteenth century that it provoked Protestant reactions.

The Holy See itself, up to the nineteenth century, did not cease to react against the excesses, distortions and deviations of the cult of Mary.

Luther strongly criticized various forms of the cult of Mary out of a fear that divine honours were being paid to a human person in a way which prejudiced the sole mediation of Christ. However, he preserved the traditional belief in the divine motherhood of Mary, her perpetual virginity and even her intercession. He saw Mary as a model of humility and faith and commended

The original wording of what is now the *Sub tuum*

Mother of God, we take refuge under the shadow of your mercy; do not lead our prayer into temptation, but deliver us from peril, you who alone are chaste and blessed.

Regina Caeli

Queen of heaven, rejoice, alleluia.
For Christ, your Son and Son of God,
has risen as he said, alleluia.
pray to God for us, alleluia.

Salve Regina

Hail, holy Queen, Mother of Mercy,
hail, our life, our sweetness, and our hope.
To you we cry, the children of Eve;
to you we send up our sighs,
mourning and weeping in this land of exile.
Turn, then, most gracious advocate,
your eyes of mercy toward us;
lead us home at last
and show us the blessed fruit of your womb, Jesus:
O clement, O loving, O sweet Virgin Mary.

Alma Redemptoris

Loving mother of the Redeemer,
gate of heaven, star of the sea,
assist your people who have fallen yet strive to rise again.
To the wonderment of nature your bore your Creator,
yet remained a virgin after as before.
You who received Gabriel's joyful greeting,
have pity on us poor sinners.

Ave Maris Stella

Star of ocean, lead us;
God for mother claims thee,
Ever-Virgin names thee;
Gate of heaven, speed us.

Ave to thee crying
Gabriel went before us;
Peace do thou restore us,
Eva's knot untying.

Loose the bonds that chain us,
Darkened eyes enlighten,
Clouded prospects brighten,
Heavenly mercies gain us.

For thy sons thou carest;
Offer Christ our praying –
Still thy word obeying –
Whom on earth thou barest.

Purer, kinder maiden
God did never fashion;
Pureness and compassion
Grant to hearts sin-laden.

From that sin release us,
Shield us, heavenward faring; –
Heaven, that is but sharing
In thy joy with Jesus.

Honour, praise and merit
To our God address we;
Three in One confess we,
Father, Son, and Spirit.

Translation by R. A. Knox

Tota pulchra es

You are beautiful, Mary, and there is no
    stain in you.
You are beautiful, gentle and comely,
Your immaculate conception!

Refrain: Come, come from Lebanon;
come from Lebanon;
come, come, you will be crowned.

imploring her for her intercession (explanation of the Magnificat, year 1, 521).

Zwingli preserved the Church's belief in Mary and the cult of Mary, but while venerating her, refused to invoke her.

By contrast, Calvin was a resolute adversary of the cult of Mary, which he condemned as idolatry.

Today, where faith in the incarnation is alive in Protestantism, the cult of the mother of God has not been extinguished. But while Protestants venerate Mary and all the saints as models of faith, in general they refused to invoke them to ask for their intercession and their aid.

The Council of Trent

Traditional recourse to the intercession of Mary has remained fervent in the Catholic Church. However, the place of Mary in Christian worship has not been made the object of dogmatic definitions.

The Council of Trent only recalled in a general way the legitimacy of the invocation and veneration of the saints and their images, making particular mention of those of Mary: 'One must have and keep in churches images of Christ, the Virgin, mother of God, and those of the saints, paying them due honour and veneration . . . Through the images that we kiss, before which we uncover and prostrate ourselves, it is Christ that we adore and saints, whose likeness they bear, that we venerate. That was already taught by the decrees of the councils, notably the Second Council of Nicaea, against those who attacked images.'

The teaching of Vatican II

Vatican II devoted two paragraphs to the place of Mary in Christian worship.

The first recalls how ancient the cult of the Holy Virgin is in the church, and specifies its nature and foundation:

'Mary has by grace been exalted above all angels and men to a place second only to her Son, as the most holy mother of God who was involved in the mysteries of Christ; she is rightly honoured by a special cult in the Church . . . This cult, as it has always existed in the Church, for all its uniqueness, differs essentially from the cult of adoration, which is offered equally to the Incarnate Word and to the Father and the Holy Spirit, and it is most favourable to it' (*Lumen Gentium*, 66).

The second paragraph specifies the spirit of the preaching and cult of the Holy Virgin:

'The sacred synod admonishes all the sons of the Church that the cult, especially the liturgical cult, of the Blessed Virgin be generously fostered, and that the practices and exercises of devotion towards her, recommended by the teaching authority of the Church in the course of the centuries be highly esteemed . . .

But it strongly urges theologians and preachers of the Word of God to be careful to refrain as much from all false exaggeration as from too summary an attitude in considering the special dignity of the Mother of God.'

The faithful must 'remember moreover that true devotion consists neither in sterile or transitory affection, nor in a certain vain credulity, but proceeds from true faith, by which we are led to recognize the excellence of the Mother of God, and we are moved to a filial love towards our mother and to the imitation of her virtues' (*Lumen Gentium*, 67).

The cult of Mary in the revised liturgy

Paul VI wanted to go back over this teaching of Vatican II 'to remove doubts and, especially, to help the development of that devotion to the Blessed Virgin which is motivated in the Church by the Word of God and practised in the Spirit of Christ' (Introduction to the apostolic exhortation of 2 February 1974, *Marialis Cultus*, on devotion to the Virgin Mary).

The feasts and commemorations of Mary

The first part of the document shows the significance of the feasts of Mary in the revised liturgy.

The revision of the general calendar 'makes it possible to include, in a more organic and closely knit fashion, the commemoration of Christ's mother in the annual cycle of the mysteries of her Son' (*Marialis Cultus*, 2).

Advent

So Advent is a time particularly suitable for the cult of Mary. It has even been said that liturgically this is the true month of Mary.

In addition to the celebration of the feast of the Immaculate Conception on 8 December, this advent period prepares us with Mary to go to meet the Saviour who comes to us each Christmas. Advent makes us re-experience 'the inexpressible love with which the Virgin Mother awaited her Son.' Moreover, just as the liturgy of Advent combines the messianic expectation with the expectation of the glorious return of Christ, it is also with Mary, as I emphasized in the previous chapter (see p. 111), that we prepare to welcome the Lord who will return on the day of his parousia (*Marialis Cultus*, 3 and 4).

Christmas

Christmas is a prolonged commemoration of the divine motherhood, inseparable from the incarnation.

That is why the Solemnity of Mary the holy Mother of God was reinstated on 1 January, the octave of Christmas. And for the same reason the World Day of Peace was also instituted on 1 January, New Year's day, 'for imploring from God, through the Queen of peace, the supreme gift of peace' (*Marialis Cultus*, 5).

To these two solemnities, those of the Immaculate Conception and the divine motherhood, Paul VI adds the celebrations of 25 March and 15 August.

The annunciation, 25 March

For the solemnity of the incarnation of the Word, the ancient description 'annunciation of the Lord' has been taken up again, but the celebration remains a feast both of Christ and the Virgin who became 'Mother of God'.

The second reading (Heb. 10.7) commemorates the saving *fiat* of the incarnate Word, who, entering the world, says, 'Behold, I come to do thy will, O God.' The Gospel (Luke 1.38) commemorates the *fiat* of Mary as she gives her free motherly consent, 'Behold the handmaid of the Lord, be it unto me according to your word' (*Marialis Cultus*, 6).

15 August

The feast on 15 August celebrates the glorious assumption of Mary into heaven. 'It is a feast that sets before the eyes of the Church and of all mankind the image and consoling sign of the fulfilment of their final hope. As I have said, in

Coronation of the Virgin. Detail. Enguerrand Quarton.
Museum of Villeneuse-les-Avignon.

this feast of the Assumption Mary appears as the eschatological icon of the church.

'The Solemnity of the Assumption is prolonged in the celebration of the Queenship of the Blessed Virgin Mary seven days later. On this occasion we contemplate her who, seated beside the King of ages, shines forth as Queen and intercedes as Mother.

These four solemnities, therefore, mark with the highest liturgical rank the main dogmatic truths concerning the handmaid of the Lord' (*Marialis Cultus*, 6).

Other celebrations

After these festivals, Paul VI considers some celebrations which commemorate saving events in which the Virgin was closely associated with her son: the feast of the Nativity of Our Lady (8 September), the Visitation (31 May), the commemoration of Our Lady of Sorrows (15 September), and the presentation of the Lord (2 February) (*Marialis Cultus*, 7).

Then Paul VI mentions other types of commemorations or festivals; those of Our Lady of Lourdes (11 February), the Dedication of the Basilica of St Mary Major in Rome (5 August), Our Lady of Mount Carmel (16 July), Our Lady of the Rosary (7 October), the presentation of the Blessed Virgin Mary (21 November), the Festival of the Immaculate Heart of Mary (Saturday following the second Sunday after Pentecost), as an extension of the feast of the Sacred Heart of Jesus (*Marialis Cultus*, 8). As well as festivals, he indicates another form of commemoration: 'Lastly, it should be noted that frequent commemorations of the Blessed Virgin are possible through the use of the Saturday Masses of Our Lady (*Marialis Cultus*, 9).

It must also be noted how 'the eucharistic prayers of the Missal, in admirable harmony with the Eastern liturgies, contain a significant commemoration of the Blessed Virgin.' We celebrate the eucharistic sacrifice of Christ in communion with the whole church, but in the first place in communion with Mary since, at the foot of the cross, she committed herself to the cruel sacrifice of Jesus in the name of the whole Church' (*Marialis Cultus*, 10, 20).

Paul VI remarks that all the great themes of our doctrine of Mary are thus brought into the texts of these liturgical celebrations (*Marialis Cultus*, 11).

This happens in such a way, as he recalls in his conclusion, that the *lex orandi*, the law of prayer, constitutes an invitation to become more deeply aware of the *lex credendi*, the law of faith (*Marialis Cultus*, 56).

The reformed book of the divine office, the liturgy of hours and also other revised liturgical books, especially the new rituals of the sacraments, contain eminent testimonies of piety to the mother of the Lord, 'recognizing her singular place in Christian worship as the holy mother of God and the worthy associate of the Redeemer' (*Marialis Cultus*, 13, 14, 15).

Mary, a model for the worship offered to God

Finally, Paul VI ends the first part of his exhortation on the cult of Mary in the liturgy by showing how Mary, while being honoured by the Church with a particular cult, is at the same time for the Church the model of the worship that must be offered to God.

Mary is a 'model of the spiritual attitude with which the Church celebrates and lives the divine mysteries. That the Blessed Virgin is an exemplar in this field derives from the fact that she is recognized as a most excellent pattern of the Church in the order of faith, charity and perfect union with Christ (*Marialis Cultus*, 16).

So Mary is the *attentive Virgin*, the Virgin who listens and receives the word of God with faith (*Marialis Cultus*, 17); she is the *Virgin in prayer*, (*Marialis Cultus*, 18), as is shown in her Magnificat (Luke 1.46–55). Mary is also the *Virgin Mother*, 'intended by God as the type and exemplar of the fruitfulness of the Virgin-Church' (*Marialis Cultus*, 19).

Finally, Mary is the *Virgin presenting offerings*: all her life, from the episode of the presentation of Jesus in the Temple (Luke 2.22–35) to Calvary where, giving the consent of her love to the sacrifice of Christ, she offers her son to the eternal Father (*Marialis Cultus*, 20).

'But Mary is above all the example of that worship which consists in making one's life an oblation to God . . . (her) assent is for all Christians a lesson and example of obedience to the Father's will, which is the way and means of one's own sanctification' (*Marialis Cultus*, 21).

Towards a renewal of marian piety

The second part of Paul VI's exhortation on the cult of Mary seeks to promote forms of marian piety distinct from the liturgy, above all those commended by the *magisterium*.

The forms of expression of this marian devotion also need to be renewed to conform with the renewal anounced by Vatican II. The revision of devotions to the Virgin must be done in accordance with several fundamental principles (*Marialis Cultus*, 24).

First, these practices must clearly express the Trinitarian, Christological and ecclesial aspects of the cult of Mary. Christian worship is of itself worship offered to the Father, through Christ, in the Holy Spirit which animates the Church, as the communion of saints (*Marialis Cultus*, 25–28).

Then Paul VI indicates what must control the revision of exercises and practises of marian piety: biblical, liturgical, ecumenical and anthropological orientations.

Biblical orientation

Marian piety must be inspired by the Bible, which is the fundamental book of Christian prayer. 'We would not want this biblical imprint to be merely a diligent use of texts and symbols skillfully selected from Sacred Scriptures. More than this it is necessary that texts of prayers and chants draw their inspiration and wording from the Bible, and above all that devotion to the Virgin be imbued with the great themes of the Christian message' (*Marialis Cultus*, 30).

Liturgical orientation

The liturgical orientation of marian piety conforms with the principle already enunciated by the Vatican II constitution on the sacred liturgy. The customary exercises of Christian people 'should be so drawn up that they harmonize with the liturgical reasons, accord with the sacred liturgy, are in some fashion derived from it, and lead the people to it, since in fact the liturgy by its very nature far surpasses any of them' (*Marialis Cultus*, 31; Vatican II, *Sacrosanctum Concilium*, 13).

We should note here that the Council called for devotions to be harmonized with the liturgical offices, not suppressed; nor were they to be confused with the latter in hybrid celebrations (*Marialis Cultus*, 31).

Ecumenical orientation

The ecumenical orientation of marian piety accords with the dominant preoccupation of today's Church: the re-establishment of the unity of Christians. The cult of Mary has always been a profound link between the Orthodox Church and the Catholic Church. But at least in the form that it has taken in the Catholic Church, it has continued to come up against reserve or rejection in those Churches which stem from the Protestant Reformation.

So it is necessary that 'every care be taken to avoid exaggeration which could mislead other

Christian brethren about the true doctrine of the Catholic Church. Similarly, the Church wants any manifestation of cult which is opposed to correct Catholic practice to be eliminated. Then, in spite of the discords which remain, 'since the same power of the Most High which overshadowed the Virgin of Nazareth (Luke 1.35) is at work today in the ecumenical movement, making it fruitful, We wish to express Our confidence that devotion to the Lord's humble handmaid, in whom the Almighty has done great things (Luke 1.49) will become – even if only slowly – not an obstacle but a pathway and a rallying-point for the union of all who believe in Christ . . . Just as at Cana the Blessed Virgin's intervention resulted in Christ's performing His first miracle (John 2.1–12), so today her intercession can help to bring about the mature time when Christ's disciples will again find full communion in faith' (*Marialis Cultus*, 32, 33).

Anthropological orientation

In then going on to speak of the anthropological orientation of marian piety, Paul VI denounces certain clichés of popular imagery or a certain kind of devout literature which in past centuries has distorted the true image of Mary as expressed in the Gospels.

If Mary is again to become a Christian model of humanism in our society, account must be taken of the present state of anthropology and psychology.

Certainly Mary lived in a social and cultural sphere which nowadays has disappeared almost everywhere. However, 'in her own particular life, she fully and responsibly accepted God's will (Luke 1.38), because she heard the Word of God and acted on it, and because charity and a spirit of service were the driving force of her actions. She is worthy of imitation because she was the first and most perfect of Christ's disciples. All of this has permanent, universal exemplary value' (*Marialis Cultus*, 35).

If the portraits of Mary are to be relevant models, they must be brought up to date to show how Mary's Christian virtues, profoundly in keeping with the gospel, are to be practised in the world of today.

If we approach the figure of the Virgin as she appears in the gospel from the perspective of present-day anthropology, Mary will appear in the different situations in the world today as 'a mirror of the expectations of contemporary men and women' (*Marialis Cultus*, 37).

Icon of the liberation of humankind

Thus in our era marked by the desire for the liberation of oppressed peoples or social classes, 'The modern woman will note with glad surprise that Mary of Nazareth, while completely devoted to the will of God, was far from being a timidly submissive woman or one whose piety was repellent to others; on the contrary she did not hesitate to proclaim that God vindicates the humble and oppressed, and removes the powerful people of this world from their privileged positions (see Luke 1.51–53). Today's woman will recognize in Mary, who "stands out among the Lord's lowly and poor", a woman of strength who experienced poverty and suffering, flight and exile (see Matt. 2.13–23).'

These circumstances cannot escape the attention of those who wish to support, with the Gospel spirit, the liberating energy of man and of society' (*Marialis Cultus*, 37).

John Paul II returned to this theme in his marian encyclical, quoting the Congregation for the Doctrine of the Faith's *Instruction on Christian Freedom and Liberation*, of 22 March 1986:

'Mary is totally dependent upon God and completely directed towards him, and, at the side of her Son, she is the most perfect image of freedom and of the liberation of humanity and of the universe. It is to her as Mother and Model that the Church must look in order to understand in its completeness the meaning of her own mission' (*Redemptoris Mater*, 37).

'Angelus' and rosary

Finally, in the third part of his apostolic exhortation, Paul VI emphasizes that the two forms of marian piety very widespread in the West are still of value: the Angelus and the rosary. By giving us recourse to the maternal intercession of Mary, these devotions help us to enter deeply into the contemplation of the mysteries of Christ: the incarnation, the sacrifice of the cross and the glorious resurrection.

Marian piety is not optional

After all that I have said about marian doctrine and the cult of Mary, we can understand how marian piety, if it is authentic, cannot be optional for a Christian. It is not just one of the numerous devotions of which Christians have a free choice, depending on their tastes and the inclinations of their spiritual temperament.

Marian devotion does not go with a particular spirituality. It is essential to Christianity itself. We cannot separate Mary from the mystery of Christ and his Church.

Granted, certain priests or faithful have trusted in the Virgin in a quite specific way,

becoming members of a religious congregation or a third order dedicated to the Virgin, or again being militant within apostolic movements, like the Legion of Mary, which puts itself under her patronage. In the Church we shall always find Christians who more than others have a devotion to their most holy mother of heaven, just as in a family some children are more attached to their mother than others.

However, just as all these brothers are nevertheless sons of the same mother and all have filial duties towards her, so as Christians who are brothers and sisters in Jesus Christ of the one family, the Church, we cannot forget that we all have the same spiritual mother, the Virgin Mary.

No one can have God as a Father who does not have Jesus as a brother, but no one can have Jesus as a brother who does not have Mary as mother.

If Mary cannot love Jesus with a motherly love without extending this love to all human beings, we cannot love Jesus either without sharing his feelings of filial affection towards his most holy mother.

The maternal presence of Mary, constantly present to us, because she does not cease to be in communion with Christ her divine son, certainly also explains the frequent appearances of Mary in our world.

The appearances of Mary

Different appearances from those of Christ

First of all we must emphasize the difference between the appearances of Mary and those of the risen Chist.

The appearances of Christ are attested by the Gospel accounts. Their authenticity is guaranteed by revelation. As the foundation of the faith of the apostles and the resurrection of Jesus for us, they are also the foundation of our faith in the resurrection.

By contrast, the appearances of Mary are not the foundation of our faith in the resurrection, and the Church does not oblige us to believe in them.

The private appearances reported in the course of the history of the Church, even those of Christ, are not guaranteed by the authority of revelation or the infallible *magisterium* of the church.

Granted, the Church officially recognizes the authenticity of some of them by the approval that it confers on them and by the cult of them which it sanctions. So it would be rash to contest them systematically. But no approval of this kind constitutes the equivalent of a dogmatic definition to which we have to give an assent of faith.

The importance of the appearances of Mary today

However, if these supernatural facts consisting in appearances and miracles do not add anything new to the Gospels, their presence today, after almost twenty centuries, does attest the realism of the Gospels which relate the miracles and appearances of Jesus.

If in our time there were no supernatural appearance, no miracles, we could ask whether those reported by the Gospels really happened.

In an age marked by rationalism, the rejection of the supernatural, the denial of revelation and even atheism, contemporary supernatural experiences confirm the existence of the supernatural and the possibility of God intervening personally in history.

Appearances today attract all the more attention in that they constitute a unique fact in the history of the Church. It was necessary to wait until the nineteenth and twentieth centuries for such supernatural events to take place for the first time since the time of Christ with such resounding echoes.

Beyond doubt these events underline the grave turning point at which humankind finds itself, in an age of scientism, rationalism and atheism.

Appearances of Mary, true and false

However, the actual multiplication of stories of appearances cautions great care. Once someone announces a new appearance, we must gently submit it to the authorized judgment of the Church and resist the temptation to see it too hastily as the presence of the miraculous.

Our world is going through a troubled period. Many people who had put their hope in the promises of science and progress have been disappointed. So they are eager for the miraculous and seek a solution to their problems in astrology, alternative medicines or far-fetched gurus. So we have to be circumspect. However, the risk of error or illusion must not lead us to deny systematically the possibility and the reality of any appearance of Mary.

Here I shall not do the work of a historian, nor shall I try to make a critical examination of appearances to distinguish the authentic from the inauthentic.

To show the significance of the appearances I shall simply keep to those which have already been recognized by the Church and abstain from talking about those which have not yet received official approval.

The manner of the supernatural appearances

I do not want to dwell on the theological problem posed by the nature and forms of these appearances of Mary.

Let me simply say that these are supernatural facts which result from a supernatural action on the subjects who are the beneficiaries of such visions. They are not natural manifestations, the objects of scientific observation or experience, like phenomena relating to the physical world that anyone can see.

Of course the transfigured body of Mary is not perceptible to our senses, any more than is that of Christ. Moreover, since the glorified person of Mary is not localized in space like a terrestrial body, it does not have to move to make itself visible. Granted, Bernadette had to go to the cave of Massabielle to see Mary on the days she indicated, but Mary herself did not have to move to show herself to Bernadette.

This question of the form of the appearances remains mysterious, and the explanations given of it are hypothetical.

With many theologians I think that the presence of the person of Mary who appears is not a presence external to the subject who sees her. It is a presence of Mary who manifests herself inwardly, for example in Bernadette, by a supernatural action not only on the spiritual faculties of the soul of the visionary but also on her senses, by means of sensations and images.

The important thing for us is to see the significance of all the appearances of Mary.

For that I shall simply cite the three best known and best attested appearances of Mary: that of the miraculous medal to Catherine Labouré in the rue du Bac in Paris in 1830; that to Bernadette in Lourdes in 1858; and that of Fatima in 1917.

The miraculous medal in 1830

On Saturday 27 November 1830 the Virgin Mary appeared for the second time in the chapel of the rue du Bac, in Paris, to a daughter of Charity, Catherine Labouré, and entrusted her with the mission of having a medal struck, the model for which she showed her.

The medal immediately had an amazing circulation. Innumerable graces of conversion and cure were obtained.

After an enquiry, the Archbishop of Paris, Monsignor de Quélen, recognized the reality of these appearances and the truth of Catherine Labouré's story and approved the diffusion of the medal, which was called the 'miraculous medal'.

In Rome in 1846, following the spectacular conversion of the Jew Alphonse Ratisbonne, Pope Gregory XVI confirmed the conclusions of the archbishop of Paris. Pius XII canonized Catherine Labouré on 27 July 1947.

Lourdes 1858

The appearances in the chapel of the rue du Bac prepared the way for the great events which took place in 1858 in Lourdes, where Mary appeared to Bernadette Soubirous.

Around 17.30 in the chapel, the novice saw the Virgin Mary, first standing on a half-globe representing the earth, and holding in her hands at waist level a smaller globe; rings decorated with precious stones on her fingers cast brilliant rays towards the earth, more particularly towards France.

Then the globe in her hands disappeared, her arms were outstretched, and her fingers continued to cast rays in the direction of the terrestrial globe; around the appearance a kind of oval formed: in the upper part an inscription appeared surrounding the Virgin's head: 'O Mary, conceived without sin, pray for us who have recourse to you.' It was then that the novice heard an inner voice: 'Have a medal struck according to this model. All those who wear it will enjoy the special protection of the mother of God.' Then the oval picture returned, and on it appeared the reverse of the medal which the sister was to strike: a capital M surmounted with a cross; above the M, the Sacred Heart of Jesus crowned with thorns and the holy heart of Mary pierced with a sword; surrounding the monogram and the hearts, twelve stars.

Report certified by Catherine Labouré's spiritual director, M. Aladel, in 1841, on the vision of 17 November 1830

As she did to my previous questions, the lady inclined her head, smiled, and did not reply. I don't know why, but I felt braver, and I returned to her and asked her kindly to tell me her name. She smiled again and saluted me graciously, but continued to keep silence. I began my prayer again a third time, hands folded, recognizing how unworthy I was of the favour I asked. The woman was standing above the rose tree. At my third request she took on a solemn air and appeared to bend towards me. She unclasped her hands, stretched out her arms, raised them and put them on her breast . . . She looked up to heaven . . . and said to me with trembling voice, 'I am the Immaculate Conception.'

Appearance of 25 March, recounted by Bernadette

'The Lady of the cave appeared to me just as she is represented on the miraculous medal,' declared St Bernadette, who was wearing the rue du Bac medal.

At Lourdes, four years after the definition of the Immaculate Conception by Pius IX in 1854, Mary appeared eighteen times. The first appearance was on 11 February 1858. During the sixteenth appearance on 25 March, the lady of the cave revealed her name: 'I am the Immaculate Conception.'

At the rue du Bac in 1830 the invocation to Mary struck on the medal was, 'O Mary, conceived without sin, pray for us who have recourse to you.'

Let us recall that the church never relies on a private revelation to define a dogma. Pius IX defined the Immaculate Conception of Mary by invoking the universal belief of the Church in this truth contained implicitly in the revelation.

However, we may note that the appearances at Lourdes in 1858, like those in the rue du Bac in 1830, confirm the traditional faith of the Church in the Immaculate Conception, defined by Pius IX in 1854.

In fact on the occasion of the centenary of this definition in 1954 the Holy See had a commemorative medal struck: on the reverse of this the image of the miraculous medal and the image of the cave of Lourdes, closely connected, underlined the link between the two appearances of the Virgin and the definition of the Immaculate Conception.

Fatima 1917

We need to consider another striking historical situation: the appearances at Fatima, in Portugal.

It was during the Bolshevik Revolution of 1917, when Lenin came to power in Russia, that the Virgin Mary appeared at Fatima to three children, one of whom, Sister Lucy, is still alive.

Mary repeated to humanity the gospel message of salvation, calling for prayer and repentance. She announced that if people were con-

verted and resorted to the intercession of her immaculate heart, her divine Son would conquer the forces of evil; she even predicted the conversion of Russia.

To these three appearances of Mary we should add those of La Salette in 1846; of Pontmain in 1871; of Beauraing in the diocese of Namur in 1932–1935; and, again, in Belgium, of Banneux in the diocese of Liège in 1933.

Without specifying the particular message of each of these appearances, let us simply try to identify the common spiritual significance of Mary's appeals to today's humanity.

No new revelation

First let us note that Mary did not offer any new revelation in these messages. People sometimes speak of the revelations of Lourdes and Fatima. This is an unhappy term and lends itself to confusion. Revelation was given in plenary and definitive form in Jesus Christ. Nothing can be added to this revelation contained in the Bible. The Church receives it, preserves it and hands it on, but cannot increase or enrich it.

As Vatican II stated, 'No new public revelation is to be expectd before the glorious manifestation of our Lord, Jesus Christ' (*Dei verbum*, 4).

Thus at Lourdes Mary called herself 'the Immaculate Conception'. But she was simply taking up a truth contained in the deposit of revelation and defined as a dogma of faith four years earlier by Pius IX.

The message of the gospel

Nor can we say that in the present situation the appearances of Mary give us new directives or stamp a new orientation on our spiritual behaviour other than that already given by Jesus.

The spiritual message of the appearances is quite simply that of the gospel. What does Mary ask through those who see her? Prayer, conversion and above all faith in the mystery of the salvation brought about by her Son. The sole aim of the appearances of Mary is to revive our faith, to make our prayer more true and to stimulate our efforts at conversion to Jesus Christ as they are called for in his gospel.

Three words keep recurring in the appeals of Mary and clearly express three demands: 'Come, pray, repent!'

'Come!': the demand of faith

This call to a renewal of gospel faith is addressed specially to our time. Mary always appears at the centre of a violent combat against the faith. Whether in France in 1830 or 1858 or in Portugal in 1917 it is in a climate of rationalist struggle against the faith that Mary manifests herself.

Those who challenge the faith radically question the personal intervention of God in history. By the appearances of Mary in history God calls modern men and women to adopt a basic religious attitude, that of filial faith in God who intervenes in history through Jesus Christ, in God who engages in a dialogue with humanity to save it and divinize it.

Because this filial faith is not human speculation but a response to the personal intervention of God, it has to be put into action. So wherever she appears, the Virgin renews her invitation: 'Come, build a church, organize a pilgrimage.'

'Pray': the demand for prayer

The call to prayer is the most frequent and the most instant. It is an anguished call which comes from her heart. Mary is well aware of the extreme distress of this world, but she knows the indispensable power of prayer in obtaining the grace of salvation. Hence her call.

This call is for both public and private prayer. It takes up the call of Jesus for prayer in filial faith, the confident prayer of the child to its father.

Repent: the demand for conversion

Mary's call for conversion of the heart takes up in the same terms the call which God had already addressed to his people through the prophets, whether Isaiah (45.22), Jeremiah (35.15), Joel (2.12) or John the Baptist (Matt. 3.2).

'Repent' was the first word of Jesus himself in the Gospel of Mark. 'He said, "The time is fulfilled and the kingdom of God is at hand. Repent and believe in the good news"' (Mark 1.14).

'Penitence, penitence!' These words recur constantly in the messages of Mary. The gospel penitence cannot be reduced to the practices of bodily mortification but is open to a conversion of heart, an intimate renewal of life, an upheaval in lives which must be directed towards the coming kingdom of God.

Rediscovering a sense of sin

This conversion first presupposes that we recognize that we are sinners before God. We have to rediscover the sense of sin and personal responsibility in a world which now tends to see evil only at the level of structures, social and cultural milieux, and to denounce only collective responsibility.

Certainly in order to change the world we have to change its structures and institutions and struggle against collective oppression or alienation. But to struggle effectively against evil we have to reach its deepest root: that of the sin present at the deepest level of everyone's heart, which affects human beings in their relationship to God and necessitates a conversion of heart.

Sin is the most serious evil of our human condition. So there can be no salvation for humanity without a moral and religious conversion.

The sacrament of reconciliation

This Christian conversion, in marian pilgrimages like those at Lourdes, is expressed in actions. The first step is that of confession, the sacrament of penance, now renewed as the sacrament of reconciliation. Pilgrimage is not complete unless penitence has been accomplished by the sacrament.

Mary is no substitute for the Church, which, through the sacraments, makes present the redemptive and sanctifying acts of Christ. Mary leads to the Church as she leads to Christ her son.

Mary helps us to rediscover the Christian and ecclesial significance of the sacrament of reconciliation.

We are reconciled with the Father through Christ in being reconciled with the Church. Through sin we have damaged the holiness of the Church and its mission of being a sacrament of salvation for the world.

The involvement of Christians in the world

Renewed by the grace of the Holy Spirit given by the absolution of the priest, we are again capable of being true witnesses of Christ in the world. Thus reconciled with God and with our brothers and sisters, we become capable of undertaking specifically apostolic commitments, but also secular commitments in the economic, social and political activities of our everyday world. So Christian penitence issues in active service.

True marian piety leads to apostolic action and to secular commitments to a better world. In going on pilgrimage to Lourdes, singing hymns and taking part in processions there, the people of God is not evading this world to affirm its faith. On the contrary, it brings its faith, its hope and its charity to life to make a new start for the world which it has to evangelize and transform. So the invitation to change one's life, 'Change your hearts', is also an invitation to change the world so that there is a greater reign of truth, justice, love and peace.

Thus through the significance of the appearancs of Mary and marian pilgrimages we rediscover all that was said earlier about the christocentric, ecclesial and eschatological aspects of the mystery of Mary, which are inseparable from the mystery of Christ and the mystery of the Church.

The christocentric aspect of the appearances of Mary

Mary does not appear to show herself, but to show us the Christ, to make us attentive to her divine son.

As at Cana, she prays for us and intercedes with her son on our behalf.

'They have no wine,' she said at Cana (John 2.3). 'They have no peace, no freedom, no love, no hope,' says Mary today, imploring her son.

But Mary also turns towards us, as at Cana she turned towards the servants: 'His mother said to the servants, "Whatever he tells you, do it"' (John 2.5).

Not only does Mary invite us to hear the Word of God incarnate in her son Jesus, but she also invites us to feed on his eucharistic body.

The eucharist is the new manna which feeds the Christian people on its way to the kingdom of God. So Mary leads us to the eucharist, as the sacrament of reconciliation.

Mary also leads to a renewal of the sacrament of baptism, evoked by the sign of water. The water of the spring that one drinks and in which one immerses oneself is the sign of the living water that Jesus announces to the Samaritan woman, that he promises to those who are thirsty and that on the cross flowed from his pierced heart. It is also the sign of the pool in which the sick hope to be cured.

If Mary does not cure all the sick miraculously from their bodily infirmities, she does lead them to receive the sacrament of the sick which comforts them and gives them the strength to sanctify themselves in the trial of their illness.

The Marriage at Cana. Detail. Church of St Nicolas, Salonika.

Ecclesial and eschatological aspect

Mary, mother of Christ, is also, as I have said, the type of the church, the 'eschatological icon of the Church'.

It is always in communion with Mary that the church as the communion of saints welcomes the grace of Christ which is the personal gift of his Spirit.

Always in communion with her, the Church gathers as a bride to prepare to welcome her bridegroom Christ when he comes in glory to celebrate his eternal nuptials.

In the same way, with the aid of Mary, the Church, led by Christ its head, continues on its way to the eschatological kingdom.

It is the mystery of the Church on its way to the heavenly country that is represented by the processions of Lourdes or the other marian pilgrimages, the processions of the Blessed Sacrament and also the evening processions with torches. Fed by the manna of the eucharistic bread and guided by the light of Christ, the Christian people pursues into the darkness its confident journey towards the holy city, the heavenly Jerusalem, the new heaven and new earth announced by the Apocalypse (21.1–2).

Conclusion

Mary in the Economy of Salvation

From the incarnation to Pentecost and to the glorious parousia of the Lord, the role of Mary is that of a mother.

As mother of Christ, the sole Redeemer and mediator with the Father, Mary occupies a privileged place in the economy of salvation.

Tht is why she has entered into our creed and remains the pre-eminent member and type of the Church in faith and charity (*Lumen Gentium*, 53).

We venerate her as mother of Christ, head of his body, the Church, under the title of mother of the Church.

So the maternal function of Mary defines her role at each stage of the redemptive work accomplished by her son.

Her role in the diffusion of all the graces is simply in fact an extension to us of the maternal role which was hers at the moment of the incarnation and then at the moment of the sacrifice of the cross.

1. Mother of the Son of God, Mary brought him to birth in the human nature which makes him the perfect mediator between God and human beings. Under this physical aspect, the motherhood of Mary already associates her closely with Christ, our sole mediator with the Father. To become man, the divine Word was willing to be engendered by a human mother in order to become truly one of us, in solidarity with all the human community which he came to divinize and redeem (Gal. 4.4; *Lumen Gentium*, 52).

2. Like all authentically human motherhood, that of Mary was not only a work of carnal generation; she enriched it in a personal and responsible way. Even if Mary did not take the initiative in the incarnation and consequently in her motherhood, she conscientiously accepted her motherhood and freely consented to it.

This dignity of Mary's motherhood sets it incomparably higher than that of any other human motherhood. Mary accepted becoming the mother of a pre-existent divine person, the Son of God, who was incarnate in her with the well-defined aim of divinizing and saving all human beings.

So Mary's motherly consent carried with it a free commitment to the saving mission of her son. Mother of the Redeemer as Redeemer, Mary is inseparably associated with the destiny of the Saviour, a destiny which led her to the foot of the cross on Calvary, but also, after her death, to the glory of the resurrection.

By her maternal consent given in joy at the moment of the incarnation, repeated in the suffering of compassion at the foot of the cross, and renewed eternally in her heavenly intercession, Mary does not cease to co-operate personally in the work of salvation accomplished by her son (*Lumen Gentium*, 61).

It is in this sense that St Irenaeus was able to write that Mary, New Eve, by her faith became the cause of salvation for herself and for all the human race (*Lumen Gentium*, 56).

3. However, since by consenting to her motherhood she consented to the work of her son, which is the universal salvation of humanity, by her acquiescence Mary was involved effectively in the fate of all humanity.

Because of this, even if she became aware only progressively of the universal implications of her maternal commitment, at the incarnation Mary welcomed redemption in the name and place of all humanity.

Mother of the universal Saviour, at the annunciation she became the one who represents all humanity saved by the Saviour. Her motherly 'yes' has not only a personal but also an ecclesial dimension. Mary, the first redeemed member of the Church, is also the first member of the Church to have committed herself in the name of all the rest to the redemption accomplished by Christ.

That is why Mary today still remains the one with whom the whole Church of the redeemed does not cease to welcome Christ the saviour and to open itself to his redeeming grace.

As Vatican II writes: 'This motherhood of Mary in the order of grace continues uninterruptedly from the consent which she loyally gave at the Annunciation and which she sustained without wavering beneath the cross, until the eternal fulfilment of all the elect. Taken up to heaven she did not lay aside this saving office but by her manifold intercession continues to bring us the gifts of eternal salvation' (*Lumen Gentium*, 62).

So we should be persuaded that we now always have need of the maternal intercession of Mary to obtain and welcome grace, as we had need of her maternal 'yes' to welcome the Son of God at the moment of his incarnation and to commit ourselves to his redemptive sacrifice on Calvary.

4. Mary is the *mater*, which could etymologically be understood as 'the one who disposes of matter'.

Just as by her physical motherhood, in offering her flesh, she offers matter for incarnation, today still, by her spiritual motherhood, her mother-hood of grace, Mary disposes men and women to receive grace. She prepares 'human matter' to welcome grace at the same time as she implores her son for this grace by her maternal intercession.

The role of Mary in our sanctification is a role of consent, welcome, openness, availability and active receptivity.

By her maternal intercession, Mary obtains for us in particular the graces of a good disposition which makes us capable of welcoming Christ the Saviour and the gift of his Spirit.

It is again by Mary that Christ is welcomed in humanity, and in union with her that the Church as the communion of saints asks for and receives the grace of Christ who grants it to us as the personal gift of the Holy Spirit.

Again with the help of Mary and in communion with her we consent to grace, we dispose ourselves to receive it, we open ourselves to the gift of the Holy Spirit, because we are made capable of welcoming it.

In praying the 'Hail Mary' we evoke before God the scene of the annunciation. We bring to bear the free consent which Mary gave to the work of redemption in the name of all. In some way we associate ourselves with Mary's 'yes' so that it reinforces ours and helps us to welcome in ourselves the grace of the Holy Spirit, just as once Mary's consent welcomed the divine Word at the moment of the incarnation and, in the upper room, Mary's intercession helped the Church at prayer to welcome the Holy Spirit given at Pentecost.

5. 'Never forget,' wrote Cardinal Daniélou, 'that if it is by the Holy Spirit that all holiness comes about, it is always where Mary is that the Holy Spirit has been spread abroad since the incarnation: "The Holy Spirit will come upon you" (Luke 1.35), and at Pentecost: "They were all with one accord in prayer with Mary, mother of Jesus" (Acts 1.14).

If the Holy Spirit was given in abundance in the upper room, it is because Mary was there; in all ages, where the Virgin has been present, the Holy Spirit has been spread abroad with abundance and has produced the mighty works of God.

That is why we have a great hope that, to the degree that our century is a marian century, God is preparing mysteriously in the Church a new outpouring of the Holy Spirit, a new Pentecost.

Here again, the presence of Mary is a pledge and a promise of the imminent coming of the Spirit, that is, the conversion of the faithless and, in our profound conviction, unity among Christians' (*Le mystère de l'Avent*).

To end this book with a prayer which can sum up all that I have said about the role of Mary in the economy of salvation, I take up the opening prayer of the feast of Blessed Mary, Mother of God, on 1 January:

God our Father
may we always profit by the prayers
of the Virgin Mother Mary,
for you bring us life and salvation
through Jesus Christ her Son
who lives and reigns with you and the Holy Spirit,
one God, for ever and ever.

Our Lady of Pentecost. Chapel of the Major Seminary of Papeete.
Mosaic by Julien Fanène.